Americans
at Work

Americans at Work

A Guide to
the Can-Do People

Craig Storti

INTERCULTURAL PRESS
A NICHOLAS BREALEY COMPANY

First published by Intercultural Press, A Nicholas Brealey Company.
For information contact:

Intercultural Press, Inc.
a division of
Nicholas Brealey Publishing
20 Park Plaza, Suite 1115A
Boston, MA 02116, USA
Tel: 617-523-3801
Fax: 617-523-3708

Nicholas Brealey Publishing
3-5 Spafield Street
London, EC1R 4QB, UK
Tel: +44-(0)-207-239-0360
Fax: +44-(0)-207-239-0370

www.nicholasbrealey.com
© 2004 by Craig Storti

Printed in the United States of America

16   15   14   13   12   6   7   8   9   10

ISBN-13: 978-1-931930-05-5
ISBN-10: 1-931930-05-8

Library of Congress Cataloging-in-Publication Data

Storti, Craig.
Americans at work : a cultural guide to the can-do people / Craig Storti
p.   cm.
Includes bibliographical references and index.
ISBN: 1-931930-05-8 (pbk.)
1. Alien labor — United States — Handbooks, manuals, etc.   2. Visitors,
Foreign — United States — Handbooks, manuals, etc.   3. National
characteristics, American.   4. Group identity — United States.
5. Organizational behavior — United States.   6. Intercultural
communication — United States.   I. Title.
HD8081.A5S76 2004
650.1'3'086910973 — dc22   2004008234

To Judy Carl-Hendrick:

the best friend a writer could have.

Table of Contents

Acknowledgments

As always, my deep gratitude to Toby Frank, for this book and for all the others. Patricia O'Hare and Nicholas Brealey gave me very astute advice on tone and balance. Judy Carl-Hendrick, as usual, was good on the big picture and on the details; her deft touch enhances every page.

Every book's unsung hero is the writer's spouse, who gets to share all of the grief and none of the glory. To Charlotte, my love and thanks.

Introduction

This book is a cultural guide for non-Americans who work with people from the United States. It tells people from other countries what to expect from their American colleagues and coworkers: how they typically behave in the workplace, how they will expect non-Americans to behave, and how the behavior of non-Americans comes across to people from the United States. For American readers this book describes how their behavior on the job comes across to people from other cultures and why Americans react to these people the way they do.

This book will help you deal more effectively with Americans:

- whether you work face-to-face with them in the United States, in your own country, or in a third country;

- whether you work with Americans indirectly, such as by phone, e-mail, or as a member of a virtual team;

- or even if you don't work directly with Americans at all but need to understand them better.

If you are an American, this book will help you understand and work more effectively with people from other cultures in whatever circumstances you encounter them.

The American Workplace?

"Of all the books that no one can write," Jacques Barzun has noted, "those about nations and the national character are the most impossible" (Kammen 1980, xvii). Anyone who sets out to describe "the American workplace" is faced immediately with two tough questions: Which

Americans and which workplace? Are we talking about white Americans or African Americans? Hispanic, Asian, or Native Americans? Americans from New England, the mid-Atlantic, the Deep South, the Midwest, or the far West? Men or women? Older Americans, middle-aged Americans, or young Americans? Americans in cities or Americans in rural areas?

And which workplace? Public sector or private sector? Profit or non-profit? Business, government, or education? The hard-hat workplace or the white collar workplace? Are we talking about the retail sector, manufacturing, financial, or health care? Is this the pharmaceutical workplace or the insurance, hospitality, oil and gas, or high tech workplace? And which division: research and development, manufacturing, sales and marketing, finance, or human resources? These entities can be entire cultures unto themselves — strange even to other Americans, to say nothing of people from outside the United States. Are there actually ways in which all of these workplaces are truly alike?

The answer is a cautious yes. If it is true that people from the same culture share to some extent certain deeply held values, beliefs, and assumptions, and if it is also true that those shared values, beliefs, and assumptions shape the behavior of those people in common ways, then it is quite possible that people from the same culture working in a variety of different places will behave in many ways that are remarkably alike. And it is these "many ways," these widely shared behaviors, that make up the American workplace described in these pages.

This is not to say that there are not numerous and significant ways that workplaces differ from each other, or that a strong corporate culture does not on occasion trump the influence of the national (in this case, the American) culture. Workplaces *are* very different one from another, in superficial and profound ways, and general statements about how Americans behave on the job regularly founder on the rock of just such differences. But there are also ways in which almost all various American workplaces are similar, especially from the point of view of people from outside the United States or otherwise raised in a different culture.

To put it another way, the techies from research and development (R&D) may indeed come from another world as far as the folks in sales and marketing are concerned — and vice versa — but their deep differences notwithstanding, *American* technical types and *American* sales reps are more like each other than either of them is like their counterparts from India or France. One American workplace, in short, different as it may be from another, is still more like other American workplaces in many ways than like a Chinese or Brazilian workplace.

That being said, most of the workplace-specific observations made in this book are more likely to apply to the white collar than to the blue collar workplace. The job setting envisioned here, in other words, is not the construction site or the shop floor — although some of the information may apply to those settings — but "the office," where people work at desks, usually in front of a computer, go to lots of meetings, and almost never sweat. Beyond that, the American described here is more likely to be a manager than an underling.

Which Americans?

To believe that it is possible to generalize about the American workplace, it is only necessary to believe that we can generalize about Americans. Which brings us right back to where we started: Which Americans? Whose values, beliefs, and assumptions — *which* American culture — are we describing in these pages? For the most part we will be describing the dominant American culture, often referred to as European American, meaning those assumptions, values, and beliefs originally derived from the early European settlers in the United States and later amended by their experiences during the first 150 years or so of American history. There are other significant cultures in the United States, of course, and people who have had a different set of experiences, but it is the core assumptions and values of this dominant culture that later immigrants have for centuries conformed to in order to succeed and prosper. More than that of any other single group, it is the worldview derived from the European-American mindset that has shaped the culture of the American workplace. It may be present to a greater or a lesser degree in different workplaces, but its influence can be felt almost everywhere.

Some Caveats about Culture

It may just be possible then, to generalize about Americans and the places they work, but it's still a good idea to be humble. People do the things they do for a number of reasons, some of which — personal reasons, circumstances — have little or nothing to do with culture. How else can we explain why two people from the same culture behave very differently in the same situation, or even why the same person in the same situation may behave one way one day and another way the next? Clearly, culture is only one of the pieces in the behavior puzzle, and while it is an important factor in almost all behavior, it will not always be the deciding factor. All other things being equal, culture will have a decisive influence on behavior, but there are many situations where all other things are not equal.

Another problem with making cultural generalizations is the fact that in many situations more than one cultural value can be in play, and the value that ultimately wins out — that determines what happens in that particular situation — depends to a large extent on the circumstances. This is not a question of whether culture or some other influence is the decisive factor in the situation, but *which one* of several cultural factors. Americans are big believers in self-reliance, for example, in letting people do things on their own, but they are also big fans of efficiency. In a situation where a manager has to choose between leaving a person or a team alone to finish a project versus providing help to keep the project on schedule, one manager might opt for building the team's confidence and another might opt to stay on schedule. Moreover, the same manager might decide the matter one way in one instance and another way in another instance.

There is also the fact that cultures often embrace conflicting, even contradictory, values. As noted, Americans value self-reliance, carefully raising their children to "stand on their own two feet," yet they are also among the most generous people in the world when it comes to charity and helping others. As Erik Erikson has observed, "[W]hatever one may come to consider a truly American trait can be shown to have its equally characteristic opposite" (Kammen 1980, 97).

Predicting human behavior, the slippery slope we venture out on in trying to generalize, is almost all art and very little science. There are no formulas, no equations, no laws. People do what they do for a variety of reasons, and while culture is almost always *one* of those reasons, it is almost never the only one. If we confine ourselves to the cultural perspective on behavior, which is what we're planning to do here, then we are bound to oversimplify. At the same time, however, we can take comfort from the fact that while we may indeed be wrestling with only one of the variables that affect human behavior, at least we've chosen one of the most fundamental.

A final note on this subject: in every society there is always a disconnect between the ideal and the real, between the values people espouse and aspire to and how they actually behave — in short, between what people say and what they do. For the most part, this book stays closer to what people say, for even if that is not always what they do, it's what they believe to be right — what they know they *should* do — and it is also how they would like to be treated (even if it's not always how they treat others).

Because of this disconnect, however, many readers, including many Americans, will not always recognize the people they come across in these pages. "That's not how we are," they may say, or "The Americans I know don't behave like that," and far be it from anyone to say these readers are wrong. No book of this kind will ever get all the details right, but with any luck the big picture will ring true.

So What?

Let's assume, then, that it may be possible to make some useful generalizations about Americans and their work habits. What's the point? Just how is it supposed to help you if you understand Americans better?

To begin with, knowing what Americans are going to do in various situations in the workplace takes the surprise and guesswork out of interacting with them. You may not always approve of or like how they behave (just as they may not always approve of your behavior), but at least you won't be caught off guard. And that means that to some extent you may not react quite so strongly to or get so upset by certain American behaviors, because at least you're expecting them. Beyond that, you will also be able to anticipate how Americans will feel about or respond to certain ideas or actions of yours, and thus you'll be in a position to act in such a way as to get the response you want.

But knowing how Americans behave on the job means more than simply being able to predict what they will do in various situations; it also means knowing what they will expect *you* to do in those same situations. The way people behave, after all — the things they do and do not do in all manner of circumstances — is also the way they expect *everyone else* to behave.

Which is where things start to get complicated. Is the point of learning how Americans behave — and how, therefore, they will expect you to behave — to teach you to adjust your own behavior to suit American expectations? If you read in this book, for example, that Americans act in certain ways in certain situations, does this mean that you should now try to act that way in those situations so you don't confuse or upset them? And if you now realize, moreover, that when you act as you normally do in certain situations this behavior may on occasion confuse or upset Americans, does that mean you can no longer act like that in their company? What exactly are you supposed to *do* with all the things you now know about Americans?

It's a good question. Strictly speaking, you have two choices: You can do nothing, just keep on acting like you always have and deal as best you can with the consequences of sometimes confusing and upsetting Americans (but at least now you'll know what's coming). Or you can change your behavior to suit American expectations and enjoy the benefits of not confusing and upsetting them. In truth, you will almost certainly do a bit of both, depending on the situation — adjusting your behavior to suit American expectations when it is to your advantage and otherwise not too painful, and not adjusting your behavior in those cases where, for whatever reason, you can't bring yourself to act like an American. (A third choice, persuading or encouraging Americans to behave like you, may also be possible in some cases.)

In actual fact, there will be times when it will take almost no effort to adjust to certain American workplace norms (once you're aware of them), times when it will take a bit more effort, and times when you won't adjust no matter what. Regarding this third option, you should always be careful not to force yourself to behave in ways that are so unnatural or uncomfortable that you end up conforming to American culture at the expense of your own self-esteem.

Let's take an example: Suppose you are an Indian software developer working with a project team in the United States for an American boss. One day the boss jokes with you about how formally you dress — you've been coming in every day wearing a jacket and tie — and tells you it's okay to dress more casually, like everyone else. This kind of adjustment, as Americans would say, is a "no-brainer."

But let's say the boss also asks you to please call him by his first name and says there's no need to address him as "Sir." In your culture it's very important to show respect to people who are older and more senior than you, to always use their last name and to call them "Sir" or "Madam." For you to make this adjustment is probably going to take a little longer and be somewhat more uncomfortable; the first few times you call your boss "Bill," it's not going to feel natural or proper. But you will get used to it, and after a while it will become second nature (and you may even catch yourself smiling one day when the newest arrival from India addresses your boss as "Mr. Smith").

Now let's imagine that your boss asks you to be sure to question or correct him in meetings if he says something you know is wrong or inaccurate. This request may be very difficult for you to comply with, requiring you to behave in a manner that is extremely impolite and disrespectful from your cultural point of view. In this instance, you may decide that you cannot adjust your behavior to conform to the American norm, that you would rather deal with the consequences of annoying your boss than have to deal with the consequences of going against your own cultural upbringing. In point of fact, you probably won't make a conscious decision at all in such cases; you just won't be able to do what has been asked of you. And that is as it should be.

The main purpose of this book, then, of explaining and describing American workplace behavior, is not to tell you how to behave better around Americans, but to help you better understand and anticipate how Americans will act on the job. If this knowledge on occasion causes you to adjust your own behavior so as to work more effectively with people from the United States, that's all to the better.

Terminology

This book frequently uses the term *non-American* to describe people who are not from the United States. This is not a happy choice; it's never helpful to define people in terms of who they are not. Moreover, *non-American* will sound very Ameri-centric to many readers. But the only realistic alternatives — *foreigner* or the phrase "people from other countries" — are not any more satisfactory. *Foreigner* is a bit ethnocentric (though it is used in chapter 1 as a synonym for *different*), and "people from other cultures" is too cumbersone and has no adjective form. This book also uses the word *America* to refer only to the United States and the word *American* to refer only to people from the United States; it should be noted that the residents of Canada and Central and South America have an equal claim on these terms (although they typically do not use either to refer to themselves).

Finally, a number of common American sayings or expressions have deliberately been used throughout this book; they appear in quotation marks because they may be unfamiliar to non-American readers.

The Plan of the Book

This book has two main divisions: Part One, The Big Picture, and Part Two, The Details. The Big Picture is a broad overview of American workplace values and behavior. After a brief discussion of the American view of non-Americans (chapter 1), chapters 2–7 examine six fundamental American values that, alone and in combination, account for many common workplace attitudes and behaviors. Each value is briefly described, followed by an explanation of the various ways it shows up in the workplace and influences how Americans think and behave.

Since some of the things Americans do are the result of the coming together of more than one of these values, certain behaviors or traits will appear more than once in these pages. The American attitude toward taking risks, to cite a prominent example, can be explained in part in terms of the opportunity theme (chapter 2) and in part in terms of the can-do mentality (chapter 3). Other topics — efficiency, favoritism, directness, certain aspects of the manager-subordinate relationship — likewise appear often, although in each instance the topic is examined from a different perspective. Chapters 8 and 9 sketch the broad outlines of two other key topics: communication style and manager-subordinate relations.

Part Two: The Details describes basic workplace etiquette, the do's and don'ts of life on the job.

But enough of caveats, explanations, and prologue. Let's go to the workplace and meet some Americans.

PART 1

The Big Picture

Land has been found by modern man which was unknown to the ancients, another world with respect to the ones they knew, which appears to be larger than our Europe, than Africa, and almost larger than Asia.

— Giovanni da Verrazano to King Francis I of France, 1542
Terra Cognita: The Mental Discovery of America

1
Americans and Foreigners

"Have I told you about protocol wafers?"

My attention was distracted by a ravine we had almost plunged into. "No. What are they?"

"An invention of mine — a biscuit that gives foreigners the know-how to behave in our midst. Which direction to pass the port, what plaids not to wear, the really important titles — that sort of thing. You dissolve one of these wafers, preferably in a little whisky, and straightaway you're clued in."

"There's a bloody fortune in it. I'll take the American dealership."

— S. J. Perelman, *Eastward Ha!*

The first thing that probably needs to be said in a book about Americans and foreigners is that the former don't really believe in the latter. Oh, they realize that there are a large number of so-called foreign countries teeming with odd-looking people who speak strange languages, but deep down Americans have a hard time believing that these people are *fundamentally* different from them. While they accept that people from other cultures may be foreign on the surface, Americans believe that "underneath we're all alike." They believe, in short, that any differences that do exist between themselves and non-Americans are ultimately insignificant.

Accidents of Geography and History

By and large, this inability to accept the essential "otherness" of non-Americans is not stubbornness or even arrogance on the part of Americans; it is, rather, an accident of geography and, to some extent, of history. Americans are born into a very large country with no other country on two of its four sides. Among other things, this has meant that Americans can travel for thousands of miles and weeks at a time and never cross a national border. Given that a mere 13 percent of Americans possess a passport, this kind of internal, domestic travel is the only kind most Americans engage in. The vast majority of the citizens of the United States, in other words, spend their entire life without setting foot in a foreign country. Is it any wonder that foreigners don't seem entirely real to most Americans?

People don't have to leave home to encounter foreigners, of course, and most Americans have no doubt had considerable contact in the United States with people from other countries. But as anyone who has traveled abroad knows, running into foreigners on one's own turf is a profoundly different experience from being surrounded by them on theirs. It is the difference between encountering a foreigner and *being* one. If more Americans had had the experience of being foreign, there would probably be more true believers among them.

In many ways, the assimilation ethic in American society has also undermined the belief in culture. For generations of immigrants, becoming American meant giving up large parts of their birth culture and replacing them with new beliefs and behaviors. The American experience seemed to suggest that cultural identity could be shed with relative ease and speed, in no more than a single generation in most cases. Can Americans really be blamed, therefore, for believing that culture must not go very deep?

Immigration and assimilation are not unique to the American experience, of course. War, famine, and disease have been uprooting people since the dawn of history, and when the uprooted settled down in a new place, they had to give up some of their old ways in order to fit in. If Americans are not unique in this regard, then, if most societies have experienced the letting go of culture in order to assimilate, one has to ask why people in these other societies didn't lose their belief in culture like Americans did.

The answer probably has something to do with the age of American culture; the United States is a young country, and the memory of immigration and assimilation — of shedding culture — is still relatively fresh in the national psyche. It is a *recent* experience, a topic that is still prominent in the national conversation. Hardly a week goes by that some op-ed columnist in a major American daily doesn't make a reference to or even write an entire piece about "diversity," "the melting pot," "multicul-tural" this or "multicultural" that, or "a nation of immigrants." People in older societies had similar conversations at one point in their history (and some countries, such as France, England, and Germany, are ad-dressing immigrant issues yet again), but that was a long time ago, and in the centuries that followed, a new culture emerged from the mix of im-migrants. So it is that people in these older societies know that the even-tual outcome of assimilation is not the watering down and disappearance of culture itself but the emergence of a new culture. Americans may learn as much too one day, but meanwhile they can perhaps be excused for not believing that culture is deep and real.

Two other themes of American culture — individualism and the re-lated notion of being self-made — likewise get in the way of Americans fully believing in culture and, by extension, in the true otherness of for-eigners. Because they place such a high value on self and the personal uniqueness of each individual, Americans have an almost visceral reac-tion to being typed or categorized, to any suggestion that there might be such a thing as an underlying set of values and beliefs they all share with each other. It's as if admitting to any kind of group or cultural identity would somehow rob Americans of the personal, individual identity they are so proud of. While people in many societies can accept that they are unique in some respects and like other people in others, for Americans it seems to be much more of an either/or proposition; either you're your own person, an individual, or you're a cultural being, a member of a group. But you cannot be both.

Individualism is of a piece with that other great American theme, the notion of being self-made, the idea that a person is not born into any particular fate or destiny but shapes his or her own future. You might be a peanut farmer, but you can become the president of the United States. If people are truly self-made, if they create their own identity, then that doesn't leave much room for anything else that might make a person, such as culture.

Many strands come together, then, to support the American belief that all this talk of culture is much ado about very little. And if there is not really such a thing as culture, then there can't be such a thing as *different* cultures — or the so-called *foreigners* who come from them.

No Excuse

Needless to say, the fact that Americans have a hard time believing in culture has a number of consequences for how they view — and ultimately for how they treat — foreigners. It's only natural, for example, that people who have no basis for accepting that other people could be significantly different from them are therefore going to assume that everyone else is just like them. And it follows that they would also assume that the way *they* behave is normal and natural, and that any other kind of behavior is by definition abnormal and unnatural.

To put it all another way, not believing in culture means that Americans have a hard time accepting that there is any legitimate reason — any "excuse" — for the odd way foreigners sometimes behave, and they conclude, therefore, that all such behavior is simply arbitrary. The strange things foreigners do may be deliberate or accidental, conscious or unconscious, but the point is they don't *have to* act that way.

This sentiment sums up the typical American view of cultural difference, and it also explains the typical American response to people from other cultures: to not take them or their differences very seriously. If there is no real logic or reason for the strange things foreigners sometimes do, then why should Americans (or anyone else, for that matter) have to put up with them? Moreover, if these behaviors are actually unnatural and abnormal, these people should thank Americans for showing them the right way to behave. When Americans encounter cultural differences, there is an underlying assumption, a deep conviction, that once they point out odd, counterproductive, and illogical behaviors, foreigners will drop their annoying habits and start behaving normally.

When foreigners *do not* give up their odd behaviors — or even agree that their behaviors *are* odd — Americans are not amused. And the stage is thus set for the drama that so often plays out when Americans work with people from other cultures: Americans find them "difficult," "rigid," or "impossible." "They won't listen to reason." "They don't understand."

"They don't even *want* to understand." They are deliberately complicating, undermining, or sabotaging whatever it is the team is trying to accomplish. In short, foreigners are "the problem." And Americans, it goes without saying, are "the solution."

Foreigners, meanwhile, playing their part in this little drama, see things a bit differently and react with that typical catalogue of complaints so often directed at Americans: that they're arrogant, insensitive, ignorant, and rude. "They don't listen." "The American way is always the right way." These sentiments, it must be said, are not unreasonable under the circumstances.

Be Prepared

If you're a foreigner, you will need to prepare yourself for dealing with Americans, beginning with realizing that any experience you've had with other nationalities has not necessarily prepared you for dealing with people from the United States. For all the reasons outlined above, Americans are in some ways uniquely ill-equipped to deal with people like you, to understand or tolerate behavior they're not used to, and this can make working with them quite different from working with other nationalities.

Americans are much more likely than other nationalities to be unprepared for and therefore to have a strong reaction to "different" behavior, more likely, in other words, to be surprised, confused, or irritated by some of the "odd" things you may do. They may also be less able to see things from your point of view and less willing, as a result, to listen to your explanation of things or to understand why you don't agree with them. They are more likely than colleagues from other countries to see you as stubborn and unreasonable.

At the same time, ironically, Americans are not very good at compromise, at finding some kind of middle ground between the way you want to do things and the way they want to, because they don't believe there *is* a middle ground. Or, perhaps more accurately, they do believe there is a middle ground — and they're standing on it! They will often "go along" (agree) with something you've proposed, for example, knowing that as they work with you they will eventually be able to convince you to adopt their approach. When you don't, they're naturally very disappointed in you.

Meanwhile, Americans are also uniquely ill-equipped to understand and appreciate how they're coming across to you. Since they start from the assumption that how they behave is normal, they assume they come across as easygoing and perfectly reasonable. They can't imagine that you might see them as difficult or that there is anything in their behavior that you would find unusual or have to get used to. They have no real reason to believe that anything they do could be surprising, confusing, or irritating to you. As a result, they will neither understand nor be especially sympathetic when non-Americans like you get upset with them. Americans are quite capable of believing that while it's only natural that they will get upset with you from time to time, there would never be *any* reason for you to get upset with them.

All appearances to the contrary, the point here is really not to put down or complain about Americans but to explain them. And a good place to start is by pointing out how their national experience has conditioned them to be more ethnocentric and less self-aware than many other nationalities. If this makes working with Americans difficult, as it certainly does on occasion, you should remember that at least Americans aren't *trying* to be difficult; they come by their national identity the same way everyone else does. That may be cold comfort, needless to say, on those days when you're completely fed up with them.

Quick Tips:
Advice for Working with Americans

- Don't expect Americans to immediately see your point of view.
- Don't expect Americans to understand how they're coming across to you.
- Don't expect Americans to think you're being reasonable.
- Don't assume Americans are deliberately being difficult.

2
The Land of Opportunity

*This was the land of promise, they said. There was no such
thing as the Impossible anymore.*

— O. E. Rolvaag, *Giants in the Earth*

*Unlimited space [is] not just an attribute of the American
continent, it is a key to the American psyche.*

— Richard Pells, *Not Like Us*

I f countries, like books, could have subtitles, then the subtitle of the
United States was written long ago: The Land of Opportunity. So it
was known in the beginning and so it is still known today. And
whether or not the characterization is accurate, whether it is more myth
than reality, it is a sentiment so deeply buried in the American psyche,
and in the psyche of people from all around the world, it has long since
ceased to matter whether or not it is actually true. The faithful believe —
and when has truth ever bested belief in a fair fight?

Land without Limits

But how did this happen? How did opportunity and possibility become
synonymous with America? Imagine for a moment an early European
settler climbing up to a spot of high ground a mile or so inland from the
Atlantic coast, on the eastern shore of Maryland, let's say around 1650,
and gazing out to the far horizon. In every direction, he sees nothing but
forests, an ocean of green stretching to the far horizon, with perhaps a
stream off to the north and maybe a lake to the southwest.

What he sees, in a word, and what all those who came after him were to see for the next two centuries is abundance. As their terminology suggests — the "New World," "the second Eden," "the land of milk and honey" — all the early observers of America were transfixed by the plenty that surrounded them. "Further down it was delightfully pleasant," a typical early traveler on the Mississippi writes,

> Here, magnificently grand eternal forests in appearance as interminable as the universe . . . constitute the scenery for thousands of miles contiguous to this matchless stream. As to the river itself, I shall not attempt a description of it. What has already been said proves its magnitude to be immensely great; even some of its branches, as the Ohio and the Missouri, are said to be classed among the largest rivers in the world. (Hutner 1999, 44)

And almost as important is what our early settler does *not* see: people, dwellings, or any other sign of human habitation. Not only is this New World vast and abundant, it is also apparently empty.

For the early European settlers, this was reality turned upside down. Imagine the impact of the great forests of New England or the mid-Atlantic on people whose idea of a forest was a carefully tended copse of shade trees on a barren hillside. Or the impact of seemingly endless land on people whose idea of a landholding was a walled-in hectare handed down and subdivided every generation. "For centuries," Carl Degler writes,

> the problem in Europe had been that of securing enough land for the people, but in the New World the elements in the equation were reversed. . . . The possibility of exaggeration should not hide the undeniable fact that in early America, and through most of the nineteenth century, too, land was available to an extent that could appear only fabulous to land-starved Europeans. (Storti 2001, 2)

How could such people help but conclude that America was a land without limits?

When this sentiment, immensely powerful and liberating in its own right, then met up with a second, equally powerful truth about life in the New World, the combination resulted in a new way of thinking that is now so commonplace among Americans it's hard to remember it was once a revelation. That second truth, the other great enabler of the American dream, was the fact that the settlers of the New World were suddenly free from the shackles of the class system then prevalent in much of Europe, a system that fixed a person's place in the social, economic, and political order — and thereby determined his or her destiny — more or less from birth.

The Elizabethan English called it "the Great Chain of Being," an immutable ladder of rank and station that began with God himself, followed by the king, and then extended on down through numerous rungs to the lowest peasant farmer and scullery maid. Everyone knew his or her place in the great chain, and the world worked because all citizens accepted their station and behaved accordingly. "God hath so disposed of mankinde," an early Puritan preacher told his flock, "as in all times some must be rich some poore, some highe and eminent in power and dignitie, some meane and in subjeccion" (Countryman 1996, 14). People could no more change their station than they could suddenly sprout a third eye, and one's duty in life was to keep the chain strong by fulfilling the responsibilities that came with his or her position. It was a world in which people did not shape their destiny but were shaped *by* it.

But in the New World, all bets were suddenly off. There was no king, for one thing, nor were there many representatives of the other higher ranks (the well-off, by and large, did not emigrate), and as the social order began unraveling at the top, it likewise came apart down through the ranks. Indeed, many of those who first settled the New World came expressly to escape the Great Chain of Being, the limits of the repressive class system, and "start over." And there, in the great abundance of the New World, were the means to do so.

Having at one and the same time the freedom to create their own destiny and the material means to do so was a truly exhilarating combination to the early immigrants who came to the New World — this is what they meant when they called America the Land of Opportunity — and this deep and abiding belief in possibility became imprinted in the national DNA. "This was the land of promise," observes a character in O. E. Rolvaag's immigrant saga *Giants in the Earth:*

the unknown, the untried, the unheard of, was in the air; people caught it, were intoxicated by it, threw themselves away, and laughed at the cost. Of course it was possible — everything was possible out here. There was no such thing as the Impossible any more. (McElroy 1999, 77)

In their book *The Seven Cultures of Capitalism,* Charles Hampden-Turner and Alfons Trompenaars report on a survey wherein respondents were asked whether they agreed with statement A or B in the following pairs:

A.   It is not always wise to plan too far ahead because many things turn out to be a matter of good or bad fortune.

B.   When I make plans, I am almost certain I can make them work.

A.   Many times I feel that I have little influence over the things that happen to me.

B.   It is impossible for me to believe that chance or luck plays an important role in my life.

A.   Most people don't realize the extent to which their lives are controlled by accidental happenings.

B.   There really is no such thing as "luck."

Out of the twelve countries surveyed,* more Americans (68 percent) agreed with statement *B* than any other nationality (1993, 65).

In the Workplace

Nothing Is Impossible

In the workplace, the consequences of the opportunity ethos show up most conspicuously in that stereotypical American bravado and self-

---

* Austria, Belgium, Canada, France, Germany, Italy, Japan, Netherlands, Singapore, Sweden, United Kingdom, United States.

assurance, the conviction that nothing is impossible. To people who believe that the only real limits are self-imposed, there are no circumstances, conditions, or situations that must be accepted and cannot be
changed, nothing that cannot be done so long as one is willing to make
the necessary effort.

People aren't always willing, of course, and on occasion decide not to
pursue a certain goal or take on a particular challenge, but Americans
have no doubt that if they want something bad enough and are willing to
work for it long enough, there is nothing they cannot achieve.

This view in turn accounts for that relentlessly positive and upbeat
attitude Americans bring to all their enterprises, their unshakable belief that they will prevail regardless of circumstances, and that somehow "everything will work out." A positive attitude is important at all
times, but especially on those rare occasions when things in fact are tem-
porarily *not* working out. At such times it's particularly important to
"look on the bright side" and remember that "every cloud has a silver
lining."

"The American attitude to life," Bill Bryson has observed,

> is remarkably upbeat and lacking in negativity. . . . If you informed an
> American that a massive asteroid was hurtling toward earth at 125,000
> miles an hour and that in twelve weeks the planet would be blown to
> smithereens, he would say: "Really? In that case, I suppose I'd better sign
> up for that Mediterranean cooking class now." (1999, 88)

In the workplace, then, anything less than a positive attitude is considered
a serious deficiency. Americans can overlook, forgive, or explain away almost any fault in their workers, but they can't abide someone with a negative or pessimistic attitude. In this context it should be noted that for
optimistic Americans anything less than being positive and upbeat —
and that would include being realistic and objective — actually comes
across as being negative.

Americans realize, of course, that people can have bad days now and
then, but sooner or later such people will "snap out of it" (i.e., become
positive again) or "get a grip on themselves" (regain control of events and
start smiling). People who don't snap out of it, who seem permanently

"down" or negative, are expected to do something about it: get professional help, take medication, or do whatever else it takes to restore themselves to "normal" (i.e., positive).

None of the above should be taken to mean that Americans always *feel* positive or upbeat, by the way, or always manage to behave like that. The point, rather, is that they are under considerable pressure to feel that way and tend to think less of themselves if they can't quite pull it off.

To the realists of this world, needless to say, Americans can seem extremely naïve. The deep faith Americans have that things will always work out and that nothing is impossible makes many non-Americans nervous, and likewise makes it difficult for them to entirely trust what Americans say. Either they're being devious or highly uncritical; either way, their dogged optimism is not reassuring.

Just a Matter of Effort

The optimistic, anything-is-possible mentality also colors the way Americans tend to view problems or obstacles, anything that might suggest that some things may in fact *not* be possible. Americans tend to underestimate obstacles and minimize potential difficulties (they prefer to call them challenges or opportunities), confident that they can overcome whatever opposition or adversity they may meet. Managers are fond of telling their employees to come to them with solutions, not problems.

This same confident attitude tends to make Americans relatively unsympathetic to the problems and obstacles of others. They believe that persistence — "trying harder," as they put it — is the answer to all problems, and that success is just a matter of will power. Failure, as they see it, is just another word for laziness, and those who do not succeed or get what they want have no one to blame but themselves. Indeed, if they do try to cast the blame elsewhere, on others or on "the system," they are accused of "whining," by which Americans mean complaining about something that is your own fault. Americans have very little patience with whiners, because their behavior casts doubt on the fundamental belief that everyone makes his or her own luck.

Listen for a moment to Brian Tracy in his modestly entitled book *The 100 Absolutely Unbreakable Laws of Business Success.* He gets a bit carried away, even for an American, but his advice on how to succeed is standard fare for American business books. "It is not what happens to you," he writes

> but how you think about what happens to you that determines how you feel and react. It's not the world *outside* you that dictates your circumstances or conditions. It is the world *inside* you that creates the conditions of your life. (2000, 15)
>
> For you to progress, to move onward and upward in your life and your business, you must continually challenge your self-limiting beliefs. You must reject any thought or suggestion that you are limited in any way. You must accept as a basic principle that you are a "no-limit" person. . . . (18)
>
> The very existence of an idea in your conscious mind means that you have within you and around you the capacity to turn it into reality. The only question you have to answer is: How badly do you want it? (65)
>
> When you back all of your goals and plans with unshakable determination and persistence, you will eventually find that there is nothing in the world that can stop you. (71)

As this suggests, Americans don't carry around a great deal of self-doubt (or if they do, they're careful to hide it, usually by overcompensating). They tend to be extremely self-confident; they believe in themselves. And they regard anyone who entertains doubts — people who ask too many questions, who see possible problems, who worry about potential difficulties, who raise red flags *no matter how legitimate* — as timid and weak. This cavalier, almost dismissive attitude toward problems or obstacles, the notion that failure is simply a lack of effort, earns Americans the reputation for being arrogant and callous in some quarters, especially among people who believe that there are sometimes limits to what can be done and situations where success is not guaranteed no matter how hard one tries.

At the same time it must be said that American optimism and self-confidence are much admired by many non-Americans. For people with drive and ambition who are always being told why something can't be done, why it will never work, or why it's not even worth trying — the "go-for-it," anything-is-possible mentality of Americans can be a breath of fresh air.

The notion of the lack of limits accounts to some extent for the American tendency to exaggerate. If they didn't actually invent the concept of "hype" (which is short for *hyperbole,* meaning "to exaggerate"), Americans are certainly world champions at it. Whether it's describing what a product will do, how long something will take, how cheaply something can be done, or how competent this team or that person is, Americans routinely make claims that are unrealistic and even untrue. In a world where there are no real limits, except the all-important self-imposed ones, to promise anything less than the best, the cheapest, or the quickest is tantamount to admitting inadequacy. Indeed, for Americans *not* to exaggerate, not to make excessive claims, feels almost defeatist.

Americans assume, incidentally, that everyone knows how this game is played, that other people realize they are exaggerating and know better than to take them at their word. They may, accordingly, be quite surprised if you later try to hold them accountable for the inflated promises they made, or if you accuse them of not telling the truth. As a non-American, you would be well advised to routinely factor a certain amount of hype into American projections or estimates (especially if they are not in writing), subtracting the 20–30 percent that is swagger in order to arrive somewhere in the vicinity of the truth.

Americans also exaggerate in the other direction, minimizing or downplaying any difficulties, problems, or obstacles that could interfere with one's rosy projections and best-case scenarios. Among other things, dwelling too much on what could go wrong suggests that one might not be altogether in control of one's destiny, something Americans do not like to contemplate. The lesson for non-Americans is to remember that whether they're accentuating the positive or minimizing the negative, Americans can't always be counted on to see things objectively, or, more accurately, to describe them that way.

A Driven People

The belief in limitless opportunity makes Americans a driven people who are almost never satisfied with the status quo, with the percentage of market share they now have, for example, or with the product in its present form. However much someone has or whatever someone has achieved, there is a sense that one can always do better. If the division exceeds its goals by 20 percent, the move is on to try for 30 percent. If they can cut time to market by three days, they must be able to cut it by four. No matter how successful that ad campaign was, there must be a way to make it better. "In America," Stuart Miller has observed, "the doors of opportunity . . . are supposedly open to all. Therefore, one is always inclined to question oneself and ask why one isn't rich and famous, or *more* rich and famous" (1990, 62). By a curious alchemy, the mere possibility of having more or doing better becomes the necessity to continually top oneself.

Hence the great, often-noted tension in the American workplace, especially in the private sector, where one of the greatest sins — and a sure prescription for disaster — is to be satisfied with one's performance. If the march of progress is truly unstoppable, then there are no rest areas on the road to success. American companies speak of "having an edge" or being "ahead of the curve," by which they mean being the first to come up with a better product or a better way to do something, or being the first to see the potential in or otherwise take advantage of a new advance in science or technology. Having an edge, and especially *keeping* that edge, is what distinguishes truly successful companies from the also-rans.

Americans very much admire what they call "passion" in their employees. Having passion means being excited and enthusiastic about what you do, but it means something more; people with passion are never satisfied and never give up. Passion turns good performers into peak performers and causes the very competent to become outstanding. Passion, also known as "a fire in the heart," is what gives you the edge and makes you driven.

Can it be any surprise that people who *are* satisfied, who seem content with what they've got or what they've achieved in life — people who don't have passion — are somewhat suspect to Americans? There is a sense that such people lack ambition, that they have somehow given up or that they are "coasting." Sometimes they are said to have "lost their edge," meaning they no longer have that inner drive it takes to excel. And in America, when you are no longer driven, you are not merely falling behind, you're out of the race altogether.

All this "drive" tends to make Americans hyperactive and impatient. There's a certain frenetic energy about them, a kind of force field that surrounds them and makes it hard for them to slow down and relax, and a little tiring to be around. You may sometimes wonder whether you should breathe for Americans, since they obviously don't have time to do it for themselves.

Another manifestation of the opportunity ethos is the American attitude toward risk. While several different cultural strains come together to create the American position on risk (see also pages 37–38, 39, 75), surely the notion of abundance and unlimited resources is an especially strong support for the prevailing attitude that there's nothing to fear from taking risks. The real risk in risk taking, after all, is the possibility of failure and all its unpleasant consequences. But if you live in a land of plenty, of second chances and endless possibilities, then how bad can those consequences be? In such a world, failure is temporary even in the worst cases, and the consequences are not likely to be long-lasting.

Americans believe, moreover, that failure can be instructive and beneficial, part of the learning process. Those who are afraid to fail won't take the gambles that lead to real breakthroughs. David Ignatius, a columnist for *The Washington Post*, writes, "What powered Silicon Valley was the freedom to fail. I still recall a remark made to me by an executive at Cisco Systems . . . 'If you hit five out of five, you won't do well here. People like that aren't taking enough chances. If you hit eight out of 10, that's the Cisco way'" (Ignatius, July 26, 2002, A33).

Mobility and Its Consequences

All this opportunity tends to make Americans a restless lot. It stands to reason that no matter how good you have it in one place or in one job, it must be even better somewhere else, which is what makes Americans such a mobile people. The average American changes jobs eight times, changes career three times, and moves into a different house every seven years.

This great mobility in turn explains why loyalty is neither expected of nor received from the typical American worker. If a worker finds a better opportunity elsewhere, he or she will take it, and the employer will usually understand (or at the very least not be surprised). High turnover and frequent job changes are the norm in a culture where people are always looking for ways to "better themselves." Indeed, recognizing this dynamic, many employers offer their most prized workers incentives to stay with the company or organization, trying, in effect, to buy loyalty that cannot otherwise be guaranteed.

This high turnover has a number of consequences for the American workplace, beginning with the fact that agreements are understood to be made with and binding on the entity, not any particular individual. By and large, when the players change, the commitments do not. This is in part why extremely detailed contracts, and the lawyers who draw them up, are so important in American business.

Workplace mobility is also part of the reason Americans invest relatively less time and effort in establishing good personal relationships with the people they deal with, especially those from outside the company such as suppliers and large accounts. If these people are going to be moving on in a year or two, then a strong personal relationship is not much of a foundation for a business agreement. It is much better to base the relationship on things that can be locked in with a solid contract, such as price, quality, or service.

This heavy reliance on contracts, and their apparent lack of interest in developing personal relationships with business associates, makes Americans come across as being excessively legalistic and untrusting and as caring only about the bottom line. They will go wherever they can get the best deal, which means they themselves cannot be trusted or counted on for long-term commitments. They are not loyal, and accordingly tend neither to expect nor reward loyalty from others.

High turnover, especially among middle management, where it tends to be the most common, raises havoc with continuity and likewise spells trouble for long-term projects. By and large, American managers aren't content to merely continue the work begun by others, to leave things the way they are, even if the way things are happens to be quite good. They much prefer to "shake things up," to "make a difference," and, above all, to "leave their mark" on the organization; after all, that's probably how they got *this* promotion.

So they want to make changes, and the bigger the changes the better, which is why the ground is always shifting in the American workplace as the latest boss introduces "new" ideas, projects, and procedures — new to him or her, that is, but often not new at all to those who remember back more than five years. This also explains in part why Americans always seem to be reinventing the wheel, spending considerable time and money on a new approach, system, or product that isn't really new or better, or on fixing something that's not actually broken. The deep need American managers have to leave things better than they found them makes it almost impossible for them even to *see* what is working well in a company or division, much less to leave it alone.

This same phenomenon helps explain why divisions or companies seem to have a new mission every two or three years, changing their course entirely and charging off in a new direction — reinventing themselves, Americans call it — in the process abandoning the previous new direction before it's even out of the planning phase. If this happens to catch flatfooted those who were heavily invested personally, professionally, or financially in the old new direction, then so be it; the American attitude is that change is the new constant in business, and people need to get used to it.

While a lot of change is completely legitimate, of course, driven by real business needs, some of it is not, driven by little more than the new manager's desire to make a difference or that general restlessness that lurks in the American psyche. Either way, while the famous flexibility of American business, the knack Americans have of being able to "turn on a dime," is unarguably one of its great strengths, a lot of that turning isn't true turning at all; it's just the wheels spinning ever faster in place.

Change for the sake of change — the notion that change in and of itself is a good thing — doesn't resonate with a lot of non-Americans, which can make working with Americans a harrowing experience. If you come from a culture where the pace of change is more gradual or where there is a lower tolerance for change, you may be wary of making long-term commitments to or otherwise involving yourself too deeply with Americans. This may explain why many foreign companies prefer to deal with Americans as vendors, to limit their exposure as it were, rather than as full partners.

How Americans See Others

As non-Americans, you would do well to remember that Americans look at the world through the lens of their optimism. They try very hard to be upbeat and positive, and from that vantage point people who try to be objective and realistic, describing things the way they are, can easily come across as pessimists. To people who believe that things will always work out, any suggestion that things might *not* work out, any whiff of these sentiments — expressing doubts, looking for possible problems or obstacles, coming up with contingency plans, or even just not being en-thusiastic enough — may strike Americans as negative or even defeatist. If you want to draw attention to a problem or bring up a possible obsta-cle, then you should preface your remarks with observations such as, "This will probably never happen, but . . ." or "I know this is worst case, but . . ." or "I don't want to sound negative, but. . . ."

Unlike Americans, you may come from one of the many cultures where people cheerfully accept the notion of limits, whether it's limited possibilities, limits to what one can accomplish in a given situation, or merely accepting that certain things in life cannot be changed no matter what. Accordingly, you may not even consider certain tasks, convinced they are not possible, hence a waste of time, or you may stop pursuing a certain goal after your best efforts have come to naught. To Americans, who've never met a problem they couldn't solve, you may come across as lacking in self-confidence or in ambition, as giving up too easily or ac-cepting too readily that certain things are beyond your control. They may think you're too quick to admit defeat and that you lack staying power.

Americans likewise don't understand people who are afraid of taking risks and who worry about failing. Such people come across as timid, weak, and cautious, as unduly hesitant and overly concerned with what could go wrong. They're not aggressive enough, perhaps because they don't really believe in themselves, and they will certainly not inspire others and may not, therefore, be given leadership positions.

The fact that mobility is so commonplace in the United States means Americans will expect agreements and contracts negotiated with the previous leadership to be respected when there's a change at the top. It also means they may be impatient with you if you want to spend time getting to know them, trying to establish a personal relationship before doing business; believing, as they do, that people come and go, Americans won't see the point of investing time in building trust and personal rapport.

As noted earlier, Americans also worry about people who don't seem driven enough, who are satisfied with what they've achieved and do not aspire to more. There is even an expression to the effect of "Show me someone who is satisfied, and I'll show you someone who has given up."

Quick Tips:
Advice for Working with Americans

- Try to sound positive; being merely realistic or objective may get you branded a pessimist.
- Don't act intimidated or discouraged by problems or obstacles; be enthusiastic about solving them.
- Never say, "Here's why this won't work." Always say, "Here's how we're going to do this."
- Don't worry too much about making mistakes (unless you've got an insecure boss).
- Try to act excited about taking risks.
- Never suggest giving up.
- Be careful about American estimates; they exaggerate.
- Don't complain or make excuses when things go wrong; just get up and start again.

3
The Can-Do People

*[Americans] treat traditions as valuable for information
only and accept existing facts as no more than a useful
sketch to show how things could be done differently
and better; [they] seek by themselves and in themselves
for the only reasons for things.*

— Alexis de Tocqueville, *Democracy in America*

After being known as The Land of Opportunity, the most common observation made about the United States has to do with the famous "can-do" or activist spirit of its people. Americans are notorious for being resourceful, inventive, and ingenious folk who never encountered a problem they couldn't solve. While these two themes are not unrelated — it's a lot easier being a can-do person if you live in a land of opportunity — they represent two distinct threads in American culture. Even if the New World had not turned out to be a land of opportunity, Americans would still have become an inventive people — because they had no other choice.

The Early American Experience

To understand the activist mentality, the notion that nothing is impossible, we need to go back in time and remind ourselves who the earliest American immigrants were and the circumstances they faced. They were Europeans, of course, and the world they knew — reality as they would have defined it — was the civilized society of 17th and 18th century Europe. There were governments and laws, towns and cities, churches and shops; there were roads, canals, bridges, and conveyances; there were commerce, agriculture, trade, and banking; the people were artisans, teachers, lawyers, and tradesmen. European society in the 17th and 18th centuries was one of the most advanced in the world.

"To understand American culture," John McElroy has written, "one must always bear in mind that it developed from the situation of civilized men and women living in a Stone Age wilderness. Almost nothing in the cultural memory of the initial European settlers on the Atlantic coastal plain of North America prepared them for living in such a place" (1999, 17). The problems and challenges facing the early settlers were not variations on a European theme but new themes altogether. In his book, *O Brave New World,* Howard Mumford Jones poses the obvious question: Their life, he writes, "was so incredibly filled with unpredictabilities, one wonders how the Europeans survived" (1968, 1999, 391). That lesson, that the old ways from Europe didn't work in America, was learned early and often; indeed, not only did the old ways not work, many of the tasks facing Americans were so completely novel that there *were* no old ways of doing such things. No wonder they thought of it not as a new country or a new land or even as a new continent, but as a New World.

The settlers survived in the only way they could: by rolling up their sleeves and plunging in. They may not have known how to do the tasks that faced them, but somehow they had to do them. Perhaps they had never cut down a tree before — perhaps they didn't even have an axe — but they knew that if they wanted to bake bread in December, then the land in front of them had better be cleared and planted by early June. The second tree went quicker than the first, no doubt, just as the second axe was a great improvement over the original, and thus it was that slowly the tanner or the teacher transformed himself into a woodsman. And the forest became a field. Through trial and error, determination, and sheer ingenuity, the immigrants adapted to their new environment, and in the process they taught themselves that there was almost nothing they could not do.

The early American experience, then — making it up as you went along — is the first great support for the activist, can-do mentality, and the other is the classic American theme of subduing nature. As they went about creating a new civilization from the wilderness, the early Americans discovered it was possible to manipulate and ultimately control the external environment. They cleared the forests — "taming the wilderness," they called it — dammed and diverted streams, and, further west, they fashioned the "plough that broke the plains." In each instance, the lesson was the same: they found one thing, thick forests or windswept expanses, and made it into another: gardens, pasture, cropland. Americans quickly came to believe they could dominate nature and, by extension, all external circumstances. If people didn't like the situation they found themselves in, then they simply "did something about it," as the phrase has it, and changed it into something they did like. Thus was born the other fundamental element of the can-do ethos: the deep and abiding belief that people can shape their own destiny, that the way things are is not necessarily the way they have to be.

Clearly, then, Americans believe in themselves; they are not afraid of problems, don't shrink from challenges, and aren't terribly worried about what might happen. Indeed, only one thing is certain: that *nothing* will happen if you don't try. This is the activist mentality in its rawest, most vibrant form, that characteristic swagger or confidence (some have also called it arrogance) that animates Americans and colors their outlook on everything they do. It's the mentality that looks instinctively for how a thing can be done, not for the reasons why it cannot; that holds that something is always worth trying and is almost never satisfied with the way things are.

In the Workplace

The Go-For-It Mentality

The activist, "go-for-it" mentality is evident everywhere in the workplace, most notably, perhaps, in the way Americans respond to challenges, obstacles, and problems. Not surprisingly, they love them. Nothing excites most Americans more, or more quickly, than figuring out how to do something that has never been done before or how to fix something that's broken — and if you really want to get an American's attention, tell her or him that something "can't be done." Americans love charging into uncharted territory, trying something new, and taking chances, and they're especially fond of a good crisis.

Needless to say, such people are not easily intimidated by adversity, not thrown by setbacks, for example, or worried about failure. They tend to see setbacks and failures as only temporary — "learning experiences," Americans call them — because they know that if they simply persist, they will prevail. They never admit defeat, in short, because doing so would mean to stop believing in oneself, and that's not in the American genes.

The other side of this bring-on-the-obstacles mentality is the fact that when all the problems have been solved and all the obstacles overcome — when things, in short, are going smoothly — Americans lose interest, become restless, and start looking around for something else to fix. They are much better at seeing what's wrong than noticing what works, much better at fixing than maintaining, and much more interested in changing things than letting them be. They want to be challenged, not just busy, and are not above creating challenges so they can have something to do. "If it isn't broken," as the saying might go, "then break it."

The belief that people can control external circumstances and shape their own destiny also accounts for the so-called "proactive" approach Americans take to so much of what they do. Americans believe that very little happens by chance. They don't wait for things to happen, in other words, or to see "how things will turn out"; they prefer, rather, to make things happen and determine how they will turn out. Americans don't wait for the future as much as they try to create it.

Even Americans don't overcome all obstacles, of course, or always triumph in the face of adversity, but when they do fail, it's in a typically American way: not with the sense that they are unable to accomplish what they intended, but only that they no longer want to. They could have succeeded, in other words, but they lost interest or the goal no longer seemed important. In short, failure American-style doesn't involve doubt or loss of self-confidence; Americans may sometimes stop trying, but they are never defeated.

Their characteristic self-confidence and the related tendency to trivialize obstacles and challenges — the we-never-met-a-problem-we-couldn't-solve syndrome — earns Americans a reputation for swagger and bravado in some quarters and for not being very realistic in others. While American enthusiasm in the face of adversity is often appreciated, non-Americans sometimes wish it could be tempered now and then with a bit more skepticism and understanding. And they especially don't appreciate it when Americans accuse them of not trying hard enough, or giving up too easily when they fail in a particular venture. To people who feel they are trying their damnedest, this kind of observation is not helpful.

Taking Risks and Making Mistakes

A number of basic beliefs come together to form the American perspective on risk. The previous section described how the notions of abundance and opportunity influence risk taking, and in this section we examine the part played by the can-do mentality. In many ways, the American view of risk — that it is nothing to be afraid of — is a natural outgrowth of the prototypical American experience of people in completely novel circumstances faced with a bewildering variety of tasks they had never even encountered before, much less performed. In these unprecedented situations, the choice early Americans faced was either to do nothing — and perish — or to try out a new behavior and see what happened. Under the circumstances, risk-taking quickly became a way of life.

Small wonder, then, that Americans regard risk as somewhat commonplace, a more or less regular feature of human activity, at least of any significant activity. For an American, taking a risk isn't something one is forced to do when all else fails, after one has considered and rejected all the possibilities that don't involve risk; taking risks is normal and expected. Hence, the relatively casual attitude most Americans have toward risk; they don't see what the fuss is all about and don't waste much time worrying about risks or trying to avoid them. Most Americans don't actually seek out risk, as they are often accused of doing, and even see the merit in trying to manage or minimize it, but they see nothing particularly *wrong* with taking risks nor anything especially commendable in being afraid of them. Americans value trying almost as much as they value succeeding, and if the United States had a national motto, it would be something very close to Nike's "Just do it."

As noted earlier, even if Americans weren't otherwise so favorably disposed to taking risks — if their historical conditioning had not mandated quite so much experimentation — they would probably still be ardent risk takers thanks to the protection afforded them by the abundance of resources and opportunity in the New World.

Along with their benign view of risk, Americans have a similarly sympathetic attitude toward mistakes. Mistakes are inherent in risk taking, after all, so it is only natural that a culture that encourages experimentation would not be too hard on people who make a mess of things. By and large, Americans are quite forgiving of mistakes, and people are not normally blamed for them unless the particular mistake was completely avoidable (hence unnecessary) or a person makes the same mistake repeatedly.

Mistakes are more forgivable in younger cultures, like the United States. Older cultures, after all, can look for answers in the past where most mistakes have already been made. But young cultures, like young people, don't have centuries of history and tradition to guide them and therefore must learn primarily by doing. And the first few times you do something, you're bound to make mistakes.

In their book *If it ain't broken, break it,* Robert Kriegel and Louis Patler tell

a famous story about IBM's founder Tom Watson and big mistakes. One of Watson's vice presidents took the initiative on the development of a new product. The product was a colossal flop and cost the company an estimated $10 million. Watson summoned the man to his office, saying there was something he wanted to discuss with him. When he arrived in Watson's office, [the man] was holding a letter of resignation in his hand. Watson turned and said, "Let you go? We just spent ten million dollars giving you one hell of an education! I can't wait to see what you're going to do next." Learning from his father, Tom Watson Jr. [always] said, "If you want to succeed, double your failure rate." (1991, 197)

Their attitude toward taking risks and making mistakes also explains in part the American attitude toward improvising. Americans see nothing wrong in "winging it," as they sometimes say, or "making it up as they go along," or "thinking on their feet" — meaning doing things on the spur of the moment without a plan or any forethought. Anything that is not planned can go poorly, but if there are no real consequences when things go poorly, then there's nothing to be afraid of.

Americans' ready embrace of risk frightens many non-Americans, especially those from cultures where one doesn't often get a second chance, where opportunities are limited, for example, where mistakes have consequences, and where failure is usually permanent. If you come from such a culture, you will probably find the seemingly breathless ease with which Americans take chances and experiment either completely awe-inspiring or utterly irresponsible. And in either case, quite scary. "Nobody dares to take any risks," a German entrepreneur has observed about his country. "You do not want to take a chance with failure because in Germany, unlike in the United States, there are rarely any second chances" (Drozdiak 1998, A13).

You can probably understand taking risks when there is no choice, when all the alternatives have been exhausted, but you may not understand taking risks before the alternatives have even been examined. You understand taking necessary risks, in short, acting when it's simply not possible to know ahead of time how things are going to turn out. But when it *is* possible, when research, analysis, or more testing would in fact reveal exactly how things are going to turn out — when the risk is completely unnecessary — taking chances in such circumstances is foolish and reckless. Taking risks is what you sometimes have to do when you're unprepared or ill-informed, when your plan fails, but it should never *be* your plan.

When the Past Is *Not* Prologue

The experience of the early immigrants imprinted another fundamental characteristic on the American national psyche: an instinctive distrust of tradition and precedent. As noted earlier, when immigrants turned to their European past for guidance on how to cope with life in the New World, they usually came up empty-handed. The past they turned to had played out in a very different world from the one they now lived in, and its lessons were largely irrelevant and in some cases even misleading. As Luigi Barzini has observed,

> From the Americans' deep-seated awareness that they are entrusted with an experiment never before tried by man derive the national characteristics most baffling to [foreigners]. One is their apparent lack of respect for other people's precedents and experiences and [for] the past in general. (1983, 231)

Without tradition to guide them, Americans were forced to be inventive, to figure out how to do things they had never done before — "invent[ing] brand-new solutions to brand-new problems," Barzini calls it (220) — as well as new ways of doing familiar things in their strange new environment. "Important innovations," Daniel Boorstin has observed, "were made simply because Americans did not know any better" (1965, 21). Thus was born that creativity and ingenuity that Americans are still justly famous for, greatly abetted, it must be said, by that ready embrace of risk and easy acceptance of mistakes described above. How much easier it is to be creative and ingenious in a society that tolerates error and forgives failure.

This may also explain why Americans tend to trust their instincts so much, why they are as likely to make decisions on the basis of feelings or intuitions as on reason or intellect. Americans talk about having a "hunch," a "gut feeling" about or "gut reaction" to something, by which they mean a kind of emotional, subjective wisdom that they are quite prepared to rely on as much as book knowledge or objective wisdom based on hard facts and data. In the New World there weren't any hard facts or data, so people were forced to "go with their hunches," to act on the basis of how they felt about something rather than what they knew about it. This is not to say Americans don't commission all manner of assessments and analyses leading up to major decisions, but they get impatient with over-analysis and too much discussion.

Americans are not merely wary of tradition or precedent, they love to challenge and debunk it, to turn accepted wisdom on its head, do the unexpected, and otherwise "think outside the box." They react strongly to any kind of blind adherence to long-established procedures or hallowed practices. Indeed, almost nothing upsets them more than doing something because "that's what we've always done" or "that's the way we've always done it." In the United States, those are arguments *against* a certain practice or course of action, not for it. Americans dismiss conventional wisdom out of hand, but call something unconventional and you immediately get an American's attention. In the workplace or in business, an original idea often generates much more enthusiasm than a good one, and if you want support for an idea or proposal that's not especially original, you would be wise to "repackage" it into something that appears to be.

Out with the Old, In with the New

Because they don't trust the past, Americans don't learn from it, which probably explains why they are always "reinventing the wheel," coming up with a terrific new idea that is not really new at all. Deep down, Americans are die-hard empiricists; they believe that the only knowledge you can truly rely on is what you have learned yourself. This explains why Americans don't take advice very well and why they prefer to make their own mistakes rather than accept the word of someone else. In the final analysis, the only past an American truly believes in is his or her own.

This empirical turn of mind also explains why you can never really tell an American anything, why they never accept anything at face value, for example, or because someone else speaks favorably of it, or because something worked well in some other setting. Americans question everything and everyone and almost never take a product, an idea, or a process

developed by someone else and accept it as it is. If they didn't think of it
or develop it, then they don't entirely trust it. While other cultures speak
of and believe in what is sometimes known as "received wisdom," the accumulated learning of the past, Americans, who don't really believe in
the past, are not about to receive any wisdom from it. "[T]he person who
discovered something in the 'school of hard knocks' through 'hands-on
learning,'" McElroy has observed, "or who created something new and
useful as a result of what he had learned on his own by trial-and-error
experimentation or independent study, was more greatly respected and
admired than the man of book learning" (1999, 107).

It should come as no surprise that Americans have a complicated and
somewhat conflicted attitude toward experts, especially outside experts.
On one hand, they hire many of them and pay them good money, apparently valuing their experience and opinions; on the other hand,
Americans tend to give experts a hard time, don't listen to them, and
question whether anyone from the outside can truly understand their organization or business. In the United States, experts often wonder why
they were hired. People in other cultures second-guess their experts too,
but not quite so readily as Americans.

In the eyes of many non-American observers, Americans take their
rejection of the past too far. It's one thing to be a slave of tradition, "stuck
in the past," as Americans would say, but it's quite another to reject the
lessons of history without even knowing what they are. This may strike
you as just more of that arrogance you've come to expect from Americans, taking the form in this instance of the belief that since they are so
special and unique, the same past that everyone else tries to learn from
has nothing to teach people from the United States. As a non-American,
you may find it tedious, worrisome, and even costly to have to wait
around while Americans reinvent the wheel or learn from mistakes they
could have avoided if they'd just done their homework.

Even people who look to the past for guidance accept that there is uncharted territory out there, some things that have never been attempted
and for which trial and error is exactly the right approach, but they find
it hard to believe that there are quite as many of those things as Americans seem to think. To put it another way, some of the stumbling about

in the dark Americans do is just the price one has to pay for innovation, but some of it is merely what happens when one doesn't know where the light switch is.

In their defense, Americans do come by their empiricism more or less honestly. That is, theirs is not a completely unthinking, automatic rejection of the past, just *because* it's the past; it is, rather, a learned behavior. It just turned out that their traditions came from a society so different from what early Americans found in the New World that relying on *that particular* past was not helpful. If today's Americans have carried this too far, rejecting even their *own* past, they can perhaps be forgiven.

The low regard Americans have for tradition and precedent also shows up in the enthusiasm Americans have for anything new. While some cultures are skeptical or even afraid of what is new, Americans have a deep and abiding faith in it, convinced that what is new is not only good but usually better than what came before. Indeed, almost the only claim that has to be made for a product or an idea to make it appeal immediately to Americans is to say it's new. You can add, if you like, that it's also improved — the phrase "new and improved" pervades American advertising — but it's entirely redundant; in the United States, new *is* improved.

Needless to say, anything that is old, and especially anything that is "old-fashioned," has no appeal to Americans. Something that is very old, on the other hand, over 100 years, falls into a different, quite acceptable category and is usually referred to as "classic." Hence the decision of the Coca-Cola company a few years ago to name its original drink Classic Coke (not old Coke) when a newer version of Coke failed to catch on with the public.

Americans are so enamored of the new that they get bored easily with anything that is no longer new or with behavior that has become habitual. They don't like to get too used to anything or become too comfortable with how they are doing things. They will often "shake things up," meaning make a change simply for its own sake, chiefly because they want to be sure they "keep their edge" (stay sharp and alert) and not "get into a rut," by which they mean getting so used to doing something a certain way that they no longer question it. Being too complacent or satisfied with a product or process are two major sins in the American work-place, while reinventing one's product or division are signs of a dynamic company or organization.

Jeffrey Skilling, the disgraced former head of Enron corporation, knew how this game was played and was richly rewarded for playing it so well. "He . . . pushed Enron to change constantly in a quest for the next new thing," an article in the July 29, 2002, *Washington Post* observed. "Each annual report emphasized a different venture that would be its next big score. 'There was a new message every year,' said David Micklewright, a managing director of . . . Enron's advertising firm. 'Because it made all these changes, it was considered a fluid and brilliant company'" (p. A11).

Champions of Change

As big fans of the new and different, Americans are also champions of change, which is practically a way of life with them. Change is inevitable, the only constant, in fact, and certainly nothing to worry about or resist. Hence, the prospect or "threat" of change, of having to do something differently or do a new thing altogether, usually doesn't intimidate Americans or at least would not normally be seen as a valid reason for not doing something. Americans might not like dealing with the details of change any more than most people, such as having to learn a new software program or having to implement a new procedure, but they would not normally question the wisdom or necessity of change. "The United States," Michael Kammen has written, "may well be the first large-scale society to have built innovation and change into its culture as a constant variable, so that a kind of 'creative destruction' continually alters the face of American life" (1980, 115).

Their attitude toward change and the "new" may also explain the "good enough" mentality often found in American business. Americans aren't as interested in turning out the perfect widget as they are in making a widget that is "good enough." After all, if today's perfect widget is destined to be sidelined by tomorrow's improved version, then what's the point in staying up late to get it exactly right. That preeminent observer of the American character, Alexis de Tocqueville, writes of

> accost[ing] an American sailor [to] inquire why the ships of his country are built so as to last but for a short time; he answers, without hesitation, that the art of navigation is every day making such rapid progress that the finest vessel would become almost useless if it lasted beyond a few years. In these words, which fell accidentally . . . and from an uninstructed man, I recognize the general and systematic idea upon which a great people direct all their concerns. (1984, 158)

Many cultures, especially older ones, are not nearly as impressed by all things new as Americans are. For people from these countries, the newest or latest thing is not automatically an improvement on what came before; it can be, of course, but it can just as easily be no better than the old, or even worse. Or not even really new at all. One just has to wait and see. For cultures that are more discriminating about what is new, the unhesitating American embrace of the next new thing is just more proof that Americans are too naïve and uncritical.

They also need to be willing to give the old more time. To many non-Americans, Americans run after the new not so much because they genuinely think it's better but because they're just too impatient to give the old a chance. To these observers, Americans simply expect things to happen too fast, so that when they embrace a new idea or process, they expect to see results quickly. If they don't, if there are snags or wrinkles that have to be worked out, as there almost always are with anything new, Americans get impatient. From this perspective, Americans chase after the new not because of any inherent value but because they lack staying power and get discouraged too easily.

A Doing Culture

It should not be surprising that people who have the word *do* as part of their national nickname would be suspicious of anything that smacks of *not* doing, activities like thinking and talking, for example, or the products of these activities, such as ideas, concepts, or theories. And it is true that in general Americans have little patience with or enthusiasm for anything not somehow closely related to taking action or "making things happen." They are a utilitarian and pragmatic people, in short, who like above all to "get things done." Start describing a theory to an American and within a very short time he or she will interrupt you to ask if your theory "works," in other words, if it has a practical application; if it doesn't, Americans aren't interested.

If pressed, Americans will admit that they can be somewhat anti-intellectual. The first Americans were too busy taming the wilderness to worry about the meaning of life, and subsequent generations haven't become any more philosophical. As noted, Americans are interested in the practical application of an idea or theory, in putting ideas to use, but they are not especially interested in ideas for their own sake and tend not to be — and not to value — intellectuals or deep thinkers. "[T]he need to master the wilderness and extract its natural resources," Richard Pells has noted,

> to construct great cities and develop a modern industrial nation, had required a practical, problem-solving cast of mind. Consequently, Americans preferred the "man of action" to the theorist, the person who rejected absolutes in favor of concrete solutions that worked in the particular instance. The classic American hero was the inventor, the engineer, the technological wizard, not the artist or academic. (1997, 178, 179)

In the workplace this preference for action and doing is readily apparent in the way Americans tend to be impatient with the "thinking" part of a process or undertaking, with analysis, planning, and deliberating. They like to "cut to the chase," as they say, meaning get to the exciting part of the work, which for them is the execution and implementation. Dana Mead, former CEO of Tenneco Inc., is interested in "results, not best efforts," he says, and

> output, not process. You can study and debate issues to death, but eventually you must take action. Employees don't like to sit around and not see

tangible activity and results. You can't warm up on the sidelines all the time; you've got to play occasionally. (Rosen et al. 2000, 343)

Americans have been accused, not without cause, of a "Ready, fire, aim" approach to getting things done, that is, acting (fire) without adequate preparation (aim). Even Americans accept that actions have to be preceded by a bit of thinking and planning, of course, but this should be kept to a minimum and should never *take the place* of doing.

The empirical approach to acquiring knowledge mentioned earlier only reinforces the American impatience with the various types of "not doing," such as thinking, discussing, and planning. If the only way to truly know something is through personal experience, by actually doing it, then not only are thinking and planning a poor substitute for action, they don't even lead to learning.

Americans are also impatient with "talk," not all talk but any talk that seems to be getting in the way of acting. They dislike drawn-out discussions and conversations that don't "go anywhere," where no conclusions are reached or no decisions made, and they're not especially fond of meetings (although they have many of them), mainly because they are nothing *but* talk. When people give presentations (more talk), Americans want them to dispense with the preliminaries and quickly get to the point. Americans don't trust talk and wait to see if people will actually do what they say, or as they sometimes phrase it, if they will "put their money where their mouth is." (Americans do believe in small talk, however, a brief exchange of pleasantries — about the weather, one's family, what one did over the weekend — before getting down to business.)

How Americans See Others

Americans think non-Americans are negative and complain a lot, which is how Americans tend to interpret expressions of concern or worry about problems, difficulties, or challenges, suggestions of the sort that something might not be possible or not worth the effort. They find people who think like this to be overly analytical, not very ambitious or visionary, or lacking in self-confidence. When people from such cultures pose what they feel are perfectly legitimate questions about the feasibility or advisability of a particular project or proposal, Americans sometimes see this behavior as obstructionist or even defeatist. Americans feel it's okay to ask questions, especially during the discussion stage of an undertaking, but not to have doubts. If as a non-American you do in fact wonder whether something is actually possible or worth trying, by all means let your American colleagues know how you feel, but you would be wise to err on the side of saying that something is not a good idea or not worth the trouble rather than that it can't be done.

Americans are likewise not very kind to people who are afraid of taking risks and making mistakes. Assuming, as Americans do, that there is almost never any legitimate reason to fear risks, they conclude that such people are timid, weak, and overly cautious. Not surprisingly, Americans are also very impatient with and often dismissive of the various stratagems the risk-averse use to weigh or minimize the consequences of risk, such as going out to do one more focus group or test run, doing more research, reviewing more studies, or sitting down for more discussion or another analysis. Americans believe there is a limit to just how thorough you can be, to how much you can know ahead of time, and they are very frustrated by people who "take forever" to make decisions and let opportunity pass them by. These people are not bold enough, and are much more interested in being right than being successful.

Cultures that seek guidance from the past and trust in tradition strike Americans as old-fashioned, behind the times, and not sufficiently open to new ideas and the inexorable march of progress. If people from these cultures don't actually resist progress, they're probably skeptical of it, and this makes Americans, the champions of progress, skeptical of them. Such people are not very creative or original, can't be trusted to enthusiastically support new initiatives or come up with innovations, are too hesitant to question the conventional wisdom, and are not capable of responding quickly to change. They will be a drag on Americans racing to invent the future.

Their strong bias in favor of action and doing and against the various forms of *not* doing — studying, deliberating, analyzing, discussing — causes Americans to view all of these activities somewhat critically and with suspicion. While Americans know that analysis and discussion are important and necessary, their threshold for this sort of thing is very low, so that when people from other cultures are simply trying to be thorough and careful, they can come across to Americans as being timid, using delaying tactics, and otherwise putting up resistance.

Because of the great enthusiasm they bring to almost everything they do, Americans tend to see people who don't quite reach their level of enthusiasm as being hesitant, lukewarm, or even pessimistic. It's not easy to be more excited, to get more worked up about something than Americans, and very hard, therefore, not to disappoint them. People who are merely positive about a proposal or a new idea, for example, or quite interested, or even very hopeful, are still missing that passion that Americans are forever looking for.

Quick Tips:
Advice for Working with Americans

- Try not to sound too worried about taking risks or trying something new; Americans may interpret your caution as being pessimistic or defeatist.
- Don't be too afraid of trial and error; Americans admire trying almost as much as succeeding.
- Be careful about too much analysis or planning; Americans may get impatient.
- Don't expect Americans to be impressed by tradition or precedent; they don't trust the past and think new is always better.
- Never act satisfied with the way things are; Americans know they can be better.
- Talk has its limits — and lots of detractors.

4
Equality for All

It's usually quite easy to identify the deepest, most fundamental values in a particular society: just look for what really upsets people in that culture. Lurking behind that strong reaction is the value that has just been violated. By this standard, egalitarianism, the belief that everyone is inherently equal to everyone else, is a mighty force in American culture. There is no quicker or more foolproof way to upset an American than to act superior, to act, that is, as if you are somehow special and should be treated differently from the way most other people are treated. This value runs so deep it even extends to people who clearly *are* special, presidents and the like, who therefore must be particularly careful to act like everyone else.

Why else did Jimmy Carter (not James), returning from his first presidential vacation in Plains, Georgia, insist on carrying his garment bag into the White House on national TV? Was it not to make a statement to the effect that I might be president of the United States and leader of the Free World, but I can carry my bags into my house when I come back from vacation just like the rest of you? A statement — and this is the point — that would go over well with the American masses? Carter, it should be noted, ran for president as a populist, "one of us," an ordinary guy from a sleepy town out near the back of beyond. He was a peanut farmer, for heaven's sake! With those credentials, how could he lose?

What other people but equality-obsessed Americans would have agonized quite so long and deeply over whether or not the First Lady (Nancy Reagan in this case) would curtsy when she was introduced to the Queen of England? Since the Queen was not expected to curtsy back, this would mean that Nancy was somehow lesser than, inferior to, or otherwise in another category than the Queen. This deeply upsets Americans. In the end, Nancy compromised and did a kind of half-curtsy that didn't really satisfy either side.

The same quality, treating everyone equally, was on display in another Queen-of-England story, the one where a startled Elizabeth II, visiting a poor neighborhood in Washington, DC, got a big hug from an excited African American lady who apparently didn't realize that one doesn't even touch — much less hug — the queen! The lady later explained that she always hugs her friends like that.

Notice, incidentally, how the president's wife is merely called the "first" lady, not the "best," the "greatest," or the "highest" lady. She's only "first," ahead of others, perhaps, but conspicuously not above anyone else.

Simply stated, Americans are not very comfortable with distinctions of rank, status, or position. Nothing — not money, not fame, not a particular talent or personal quality, not even success — makes one better than anyone else. These things just make a person different, and every American is indeed very proud of how different he or she is from every other American (that other great value, individualism). But make no mistake: even as Americans insist on their individual differences, they insist even more that they should never be *treated* differently.

Americans "bristle at any system of arbitrary social ranking independent of achievement," Edward T. Hall has written.

> They are uncomfortable with class systems such as those in France or England. The American belief in equality makes Americans dislike those who act superior or condescending. Even influential people usually make an effort to appear approachable. For example, the manager who puts his feet on the desk, works in his shirt-sleeves, and invites everyone to call him by his first name is trying to show that he too is a member of the team. (1990, 150)

Not surprisingly, the vernacular is riddled with expressions, none of them very kind, to describe people who violate this most American of

American values. Such people are "too big for their britches," "have a big head," or a person's position "has gone to her head." They "put on airs," have "forgotten where they came from" (i.e., down here with the rest of us), "put their trousers on one leg at a time" (like everyone else), and occasionally have to be "cut down to size" (i.e., the size of the rest of us). "Who does he think he is?" Americans sometimes ask of such people (and, tellingly, they used to add, "the king of England?").

This is not to say Americans don't look up to or respect certain people or look down on and disparage others. They do, but they still try to treat people in both categories the same. And if someone an American looks up to starts acting "superior," that person will quickly lose respect. Note, for example, the furor that was ignited not so long ago at a Washington, DC, movie theater when it appeared that the management had reserved seats to an evening showing of *The Quiet American* for Ted Koppel, a well-known American news personality, and members of his family. "Why should anyone have special privileges and be able to have reserved seats," one reader wrote to *The Washington Post*. "I thought Koppel tried to represent equality in this country, [but] evidently not when it comes to himself or his family" (February 12, 2003, C3). This sentiment is shared by another annoyed reader who explained that "the whole point of America is that there is no class system." The final word must go to the woman who wrote in to explain that

> for the record, I am a quiet American who mows my own lawn, mops my own floor, and knows I have to get to a popular movie early in order to get good seats . . . I wish all these self-entitled celebrities and their sycophantic toadies would move to France. (*The Washington Post*, February 12, 2003, C3)

Koppel, naturally, responded by saying he had never asked for reserved seats but that they had been offered to him by the management (which, presumably, has since moved to France).

It should not come as a surprise that egalitarianism runs so deep in the American psyche. Many of the earliest immigrants to America were escaping European cultures where people were judged and treated according to their social class, their position in a rigid social hierarchy. You were born into your place in that social order, which could not be changed and which effectively determined your future. And your well-being was largely a matter of "knowing your place," your location in the hierarchy, and never acting above it (or below it, for that matter). It is not surprising that people yearning to escape systematic *in*equality would place equality at the center of the new ethos they were creating. As noted elsewhere, "You didn't leave the safety and security of home and sail across the North Atlantic to utterly alien shores merely to recreate there a way of life you found unbearable in Europe" (Storti 2001, 15).

In the Workplace

Bosses and Subordinates

In the workplace, the equality value is probably most evident in the way bosses and subordinates relate to each other, and especially in the expectations each has of how the other should behave. This topic is discussed in detail elsewhere (see chapter 9, Of Bosses and Subordinates); suffice it to say here that bosses generally try to err on the side of treating subordinates as equals, not because boss and subordinate have equal power, authority, or responsibility — for they do not — but in the sense that having more of all those things doesn't automatically make a boss better than or somehow superior to his or her subordinates.

While bosses are expected to be relatively casual and informal with their subordinates, wearing their authority lightly, for their part subordinates tend to be slightly less casual and more formal with their bosses. Everyone understands that bosses are not just another member of the team, in other words, even though they may act as if they are. There's not an entirely separate code of conduct for bosses and for peers — subordinates tend to be casual and informal with both — but there are differences in degree. Subordinates treat bosses with more respect, for example, and are more careful of what they say around them. At the same time, it's important not to overdo it with one's boss, treating him or her with elaborate courtesy or deference; likewise, it's very important for a boss not to expect that kind of subservience. It is true, incidentally, that in the presence of outsiders or visitors, Americans tend to treat their bosses more formally.

No one, especially bosses, should ever act as if he or she is "above" any particular task, that there are certain things a person in a high-level position simply never does. As a practical matter, the division chief probably never does clean up the copy room, and the CEO doesn't serve coffee or move furniture. But for these people to act as if they *should* never do these things, as if they are somehow "too good" to do these things (as Americans would put it), this would be very bad form. If everybody's equal, then no one is too good for anything.

Equality in Action

In a related matter, non-Americans should always be sure to thank people who render them any kind of service, no matter how small, even if rendering that service is that person's job. Thanking someone for doing what they're supposed to do, for what they're paid to do, is not condescending or patronizing to an American; it's merely a tacit acknowledgment that no one is automatically owed or inherently deserving of any particular treatment. If people treat you politely or with respect, in other words, it's not because they have to; it's because they freely choose to, and saying thank you merely acknowledges this fact.

Americans thank the person who bags their groceries, who brings them their entrée, who cuts their hair, opens the door, parks their car, shines their shoes, empties their waste basket, and delivers their mail. They may pay for many of these services, but that doesn't mean they shouldn't show their gratitude. This phenomenon explains one of the most common cultural observations people from other cultures make about Americans: that they're always saying "Thank you," often for the most trivial of reasons.

The equality norm also explains, at least in part, the American attitude toward titles. Americans don't put much stock in titles or use them very much because titles identify distinctions, whether in level of education or level of power, and Americans are uncomfortable with distinctions. Americans may be as proud of their achievements, their distinctions, as people from other cultures, but they're careful not to act proud, and they are likewise extremely quick to pick up on any lapse from humility. People who insist on using their title — especially those who insist on *other* people using their title — are ridiculed. Using titles appears to demand respect, and respect cannot be demanded from Americans; it can only be earned.

Fairness and Favoritism

Fairness is another bedrock value in the American workplace, and favoritism, which violates that value, is therefore one of the worst transgressions. Bosses are very concerned about being fair, and their subordinates are, if anything, even more concerned. "Fairness is a national pastime," Robert Rosen, Patricia Digh, Marshall Singer, and Carl Phillips have written, "and whole industries are built around protecting the underdog" (2000, 319). Fairness American-style means to be completely impartial, treating all subordinates the same regardless of circumstances or their position, applying rules and regulations equally, and judging everyone by the same standards.

Almost nothing undermines office morale and performance more quickly than favoritism. Whether it comes in the form of making exceptions or allowances for certain people or giving certain people preferential treatment, favoritism inevitably suggests that some people are somehow more equal than others, and this is anathema to most Americans. Bosses *have* favorites, of course, like everyone else, but they know better than to "let it show," to appear to be letting personal preferences influence how they treat those who work for them.

Avoiding even the appearance of favoritism is especially important in selecting someone for a job or in awarding a contract. While the individual doing the selecting may have a personal preference, he or she will be careful to base the selection as much as possible on such nominally objective criteria as experience, skills, and professional background, creating what is sometimes referred to as "a level playing field." In some organizations, particularly in the government sector, the names of job applicants are even removed from the application during the initial evaluation stage to enable a so-called "blind" evaluation of each person's credentials.

The fairness ethic extends beyond employees to embrace how the public in general is to be treated, such as clients or customers, vendors, and contractors. The main principle here once again is that businesses or organizations should treat everyone they deal with in the same manner, applying rules and regulations impartially, regardless of a person's rank, social status, personal relationship to the provider, "connections," or any other criteria that could be deemed subjective or discriminatory. People who try to "pull rank," demanding special treatment because of who they are, are looked down upon, and employees who give in to such requests will generally not be rewarded. The story is told of a quick-thinking airline employee who was checking in a flight when a man, ignoring the long line, rushed up to her and demanded to be served. When she told the man he would have to get in line, he shouted, "Do you have any idea who I am?" Whereupon the woman got on the public address system and calmly announced to the entire concourse that there was a man at gate B26 who didn't know who he was and asked anyone who could help identify him to please come forward.

Evaluating Employees

Treating everyone the same explains in part why performance, and especially "results," is practically the sole measure Americans use to evaluate an employee's worth and determine who gets retained and promoted and who does not (see chapter 5 for more on this topic). If everyone is equal, the fairest way to distinguish among equals is to use the most objective, quantifiable, and transparent criterion possible, and for most workplaces that's performance. So it is that Americans go to great, sometimes even comic lengths (at least outwardly) to avoid applying any other criteria, anything that could be perceived as subjective — such as attitude, work habits, interpersonal skills — in evaluating employees. In the process, of course, employees who have *nothing but* results to recommend them — and any number of less encouraging, albeit intangible strikes against them — often fare rather better than colleagues who have, in the vernacular, somewhat less to "*show* for themselves."

Whether it's altogether fair or not, limiting the criteria for employee evaluation in this way is often the safest and most prudent course in what is, after all, the world's most litigious society. "You can't argue with results," Americans like to say, and one can't help but wonder if the great emphasis and faith Americans place on results are not driven as much by a desire to avoid the argument as to reward the performance.

This same phenomenon, evaluating and rewarding employees primarily on the basis of objective, quantifiable criteria, may also explain why the people who move up and become managers in America so often lack the skills they need to be good leaders. Many of these leadership skills, after all — vision, charisma, communication skills, people skills — are just the kind of fuzzy, subjective indicators Americans try to stay away from.

These statements are something of an oversimplification, of course; it's not that Americans do not value the workplace intangibles, anything that can't be measured or quantified, or that they don't take into account or reward anything except results. Americans understand that an employee's worth and contribution to an organization comes in many forms, and they appreciate all of them. But it is true that they tend to err in favor of rewarding results more than people in many other cultures, and the reason, at least in part, is the fear of making what might appear to be arbitrary distinctions among people who are, after all, inherently equal.

For the record we should note that while Americans generally believe in and aspire to a fair, favoritism-free workplace, they don't always pull it off. Some people *do* get treated better than others in the United States; who you know *is* important and the playing field is *not* always perfectly level. The point is not so much that people in other countries play favorites and Americans do not, but rather that Americans know better than to play favorites and feel bad when they do. It's also a matter of degree; while there is certainly favoritism in the American workplace, there is probably less than in many other cultures (especially the so-called particularist cultures described in the following section).

How Americans See Others

As noted at the beginning of this section, Americans have a very good nose for people who act superior, who seem to violate in any way the notion that we're all equal. Managers and bosses have to be watched especially carefully in this regard, and non-American bosses who expect to be treated with elaborate courtesy or deference may come across as pompous or arrogant. Certainly anyone, boss or otherwise, who acts as if he or she is somehow too important or "above" doing certain office tasks, especially more menial jobs that a person might feel are below his or her station, will not be respected.

Americans do not respond well to being treated unfairly (according to their definition of fairness), and they will be especially upset if one person, one contractor, one vendor is given preferential treatment over another. They react quite unfavorably to what they call a "double standard" or "situational ethics," by which they mean applying one set of standards in one situation (involving, say, a family member) and another set in another situation (involving someone they don't know or are not beholden to). Americans believe the same standards should be applied in all situations; that's why it's called a standard!

It is for this reason that Americans have a very hard time with so-called particularist cultures, where people distinguish clearly between and have entirely different standards for treating their "ingroup" (extended family and very close friends) and their "outgroup" (everybody else), taking very good care of members of the former and having no obligations to or responsibilities for members of the latter (who have their own ingroup to look after them). In such societies, being objective and impartial have no place; everyone knows life isn't fair, and people don't expect to be treated equally. What they *do* expect is to be treated very well by everyone in their ingroup, to be given preferential treatment, to have exceptions made for them, and generally to be accorded every advantage possible over outgroup members.

In a study done in Ghana, civil servants were asked what they would do if they reported to work one morning and found a relative among the group of people waiting to be served. Eighty percent said they would feel obliged to serve their relative first, and 92.6 percent said that this is what the relative would expect. The study noted that the

> civil servants who replied were inclined to feel that in such situations their relatives would not understand the formal requirements of their job and would be likely to see them as bad, hard-hearted, and generally selfish and uncaring if they did not help their family. (Hickson and Pugh 1995, 238)

For Americans this kind of behavior borders on nepotism, which is frowned upon in the workplace and even considered unethical by some. "Right is right," Americans are fond of saying, "whatever the circumstances" (universalism). Needless to say, particularists find the American habit of not making exceptions or allowances for family members, of not looking after one's own, as callous and disloyal. Indeed, by particularist logic, it's the epitome of unfairness!

Finally, Americans used to being rewarded and promoted primarily for their performance may be surprised when people from other cultures apply a wider range of criteria in evaluating employees. They may wonder, for example, how someone who's not very efficient, not a high achiever, or simply "too nice" ever got into an authority position or why such a nonperformer, whether promoted or not, is retained in the organization or division. And Americans may likewise be surprised when their own results are not by themselves enough to enable them to advance. If they are judged by their attitude, for example, or by their work habits, or according to whether or not they get along well with their coworkers — if they are judged by these intangibles and/or see others being judged in this way, they may not understand and, in their own case, they may even object.

Quick Tips:

Advice for Working with Americans

- If you're a boss, don't play favorites, obviously treating some subordinates better than others.
- Don't expect people to use your title or insist that they do.
- Try to judge everyone by the same standards, which should be as objective and transparent as possible (such as results or performance).
- Always thank people when they render you a service, even if they're just doing their job.
- Never act superior, as if you are too important or above doing something.

5
You Are What You've Done

*There is perhaps not a more dangerous Error than
to believe we are bound to reverence men for the
Offices they sustain without any Regard
to their . . . useful Actions.*

— William Livingstone, *People of Paradox*

Americans often speak of "inventing" or "reinventing" themselves. As noted elsewhere, the social, financial, and professional limits of the European feudal/class system gradually lost their hold over the common man and woman in the New World. Accordingly, early Americans were born without any particular destiny and were in theory free to become whomever and whatever they wanted — or at least free to try. They were, as the famous phrase put it, "self-made," with nothing but hard work standing between themselves and their dreams. That sentiment has always been something of an exaggeration, of course, true in general but not always true in particular — and certainly more true for some Americans than for others. But all in all, the possibility of being self-made was probably more real for people in the New World than in the world they left behind.

People who are not born with any particular identity, into a certain social class, for example, or a certain trade or profession — people who are not defined from without, as it were — are left to define themselves. And so it was that in the New World a person's achievements, what he or she did, became a person's identity: who he or she was. Americans came to define themselves by the sum of their achievements, and these quickly became the measure of an individual's worth, the criteria by which people came to judge themselves and others.

The Drive to Achieve

And it remains so to this day. To most Americans, a successful person is first and foremost someone who has accomplished a great deal, the so-called "high achievers," people who have "something to show" for their efforts (and they also speak of under- and over-achievers). Americans admire, look up to, and want to be like such people; likewise, they admire the qualities it takes to become a high achiever, which reads like a list of the top American values: ambition, aggressiveness, never being satisfied or taking no for an answer, being driven and competitive, never giving up. They like people who, as the saying goes, "get the job done," "make things happen," and "get results."

Above all, America is a culture of doing. If you have "done well," it is a source of pride and satisfaction; if you could have "done better," it gnaws at you. Not surprisingly, the regular reviews bosses are expected to give employees are called "performance evaluations," making it quite clear that it's performance — not personality, loyalty, intellect, attitude, dedication, commitment, etc. — that really counts.

Ambition

The achievement ethic is what makes ambition such a core value in American culture — and laziness one of the worst sins. Ambition is the driver behind achievement, what pushes people to succeed, or at least to try, and anyone who is ambitious gets respect. Being ambitious — *wanting* to succeed — is almost as good as actually succeeding. Americans can understand and forgive someone who "tries," someone who wants to succeed but somehow doesn't quite manage. What they can't understand or forgive is someone who is lazy, who doesn't even care about succeeding.

The emphasis on ambition explains in part why Americans look up to people who don't seem to have much else to recommend them, people who aren't especially pleasant, for example, or intelligent, someone you might want to meet or have over to dinner. What matters is that these people made it to the top, and it's what it takes to get there — the drive, the passion, the ambition — that Americans admire. And it is those who apparently have the greatest drive, symbolized by beating out everyone else and getting to the top, who are the most admired. "Nice guys finish last," Americans say, meaning that it's more important to be successful than to be a pleasant or likable person (or at least that the two don't usually go together).

Americans don't automatically admire people "at the top," by the way; it all depends on how you got there. Success and the respect that goes with it have to be "earned," through hard work. If you were born at the top, into a wealthy family or to famous parents, you have to prove yourself by not trading on your connections, for example, or by refusing to take money from your family and going off to "make it on your own." The achievement ethic, in short, demands achievements, and having the good fortune to be born into wealth and privilege is not an accomplishment. It doesn't say anything about you, meaning it doesn't indicate one way or another if "you've got what it takes" — i.e., our old friend ambition.

The true heroes in American culture, then, are not those who start at the top but those who have to "work their way" up there, preferably against all odds. And the greater the odds — the harder the person has to work — the more he or she is admired. The quintessential American story, after all, is "rags to riches," not "riches to more riches."

Competition

Competition is another central piece of the achievement ethic. In a society of self-made individuals, where people derive self-respect and the respect of others in large part from their accomplishments, there is an inevitable, inherent pressure to be the person or the company or the division with the *most* accomplishments — hence the habit of judging one's own worth by the standard of what others have achieved, and then trying to exceed it. This is why winning, and not merely doing well or doing one's best, is so important to Americans; if you win, then *you* set the standard. Even when there is no one to compete with, Americans will still compete with themselves, in the sense that they are never satisfied with what they have achieved. How is it possible, after all, to have too much self-esteem?

Americans go out of their way not to behave like this, incidentally, to not judge people solely by their achievements or how much money they make, as if suspecting that somehow this is wrong (or at least that it looks bad). So they bend over backwards to point out that so-and-so is a "nice person," "a good mother," "tries hard," or has a "positive attitude." But don't waste your time looking for people like this "at the top." Indeed, as soon as you hear board members saying the CEO "tries hard" and has a "positive attitude," you can be sure they're already interviewing his or her replacement. Americans may know better than to judge people by what they've done or how much money they make, but in the end they can't help themselves.

The Bottom Line

One of the easiest ways to measure achievement, of course, is in terms of money, and it should come as no surprise that Americans are somewhat obsessed with money. Americans talk endlessly about what they call "the bottom line," otherwise known as profit, and in the private sector at least, profit is both literally and figuratively the bottom line — the ultimate standard for measuring results and performance. Whatever else they may say, the only results Americans really care about are those that increase revenue, and the only performance that really matters is that of the stock price.

In the private sector, every major decision is based to a large extent on the impact on what is known as "the profit picture." Careers rise and fall based on profit; executive salaries are pegged to stock price, market share, or return on investment (ROI): the fortunes of entire divisions and whole companies can be changed by one or two quarterly earnings reports. It may devastate the local economy in Missoula or Islip, but if sending a thousand jobs to Mexico improves profit margins, the decision is almost a no-brainer. While corporations in many countries acknowledge social obligations to the communities they are located in, American companies worry chiefly about stockholders.

Materialism

The achievement ethos and the importance of making money also help explain that great American preoccupation with things, the materialist mentality. In the view of many non-Americans, Americans are notorious for being materialistic, for deriving deep and lasting satisfaction and even self-respect from the acquisition of possessions. The favorite American pastime is apparently shopping, which in turn makes "sales" one of the most important events in contemporary American life (right after overeating).

In point of fact, Americans care very little for things per se; indeed, they are constantly replacing, upgrading, or simply throwing away most of what they own. What they actually care about — why they feel so compelled to acquire things — is what the ability to have things says about a person. Having things, especially nice things and expensive things, means you can afford them, and if you can afford them, that must mean you are successful. And it is the success, of which things are merely the visible manifestation, that really matters.

The Meaning of Work

The high value Americans place on achievement explains to a large extent their attitude toward work. Americans are famous for being workaholics, and while the charge is something of an oversimplification, it does stand up well to scrutiny. On average, Americans in the manufacturing sector work 320 more hours a year — a total of two months — than their counterparts in Germany and France. The average vacation allowance in most European countries is a minimum of four weeks, versus the American average of two. In 1990, Americans reported that their free time had decreased 40 percent since 1973.

People work for a lot of reasons, and not all workaholics fit the same profile. But it should not be surprising that people work long hours in a culture where their identity and sense of self-worth are to a large extent a product of what they have achieved. After all, if achievement is such a good thing, then work — which is the means to achievement — is also a good thing. And *more* work, of course, nights and on weekends, is an even better thing. Endowed with such a lofty purpose, work in and of itself becomes satisfying, even fulfilling.

Whether or not they actually admire workaholics, most Americans understand the underlying impulse. Extolling work as they do, they are culturally disposed to look favorably on people who work hard and to look askance at those who do not, wondering whether the latter have enough ambition, whether they care sufficiently about "getting ahead" or "bettering themselves," whether or not they are, in a word, lazy. For reasons that should by now be obvious, to be accused of being lazy is one of the worst things that can be said about an American.

It is in part the fear of just such an accusation and the negative consequences it can lead to that drives many Americans to work even harder than they otherwise might. Next to a workaholic, after all, someone who merely works very hard can easily come across as a slacker. In her book *The Overworked American*, Juliet Schorr describes the phenomenon:

> [H]owever strong this cultural predisposition to hard work, "workaholism" is to some extent a creation of the system, rather than its cause. As long as there are even a few workaholics, competition will force others to keep up. Employers will prefer the hard workers, and these will win out over their colleagues who, either out of personal preference or because they have family responsibilities, do not put in the hours. One engineer noted, "I don't like to put in 80-hour weeks, but a lot of people do. And those are the people who get the projects and the promotions." This suggests that the workaholic can set the standard to which others are compelled to adhere. (1993, 70)

Leisure

The high premium they place on work makes Americans naturally wary of anything that smacks of "not work," such as idleness and leisure time, which is part of why Americans go to such great lengths to stay busy. If work is good, then leisure is problematic, especially too much leisure. Americans do often complain about the meager two weeks of vacation time they get annually, but at the same time leisure in excess leaves a person wide open to the charge of being lazy or simply not ambitious. Schorr talks elsewhere in her book about the American "cultural imperative . . . that says that men with leisure are lazy" (159). She goes on to describe the

> historical precedent for the idea that Americans are obsessed with work; as early as 1648, Massachusetts legislated idleness a punishable crime. There is no denying what the historian Daniel Rodgers described as the

nation's tendency to "the elevation of work over leisure . . . an ethos that permeated life and manners." (70)

It's worth noting in this context the phrase Americans most often use to describe those who do not work: "the idle rich." Clearly it is their idleness, not their riches, that condemns them.

In another book, *Working At Play,* a history of vacations in the United States, Cindy Aron notes that Americans have struggled for at least 150 years with the "persistent dilemma" of

> [h]ow to enjoy leisure without jeopardizing the commitment to work. What is compelling about the history of vacations is the constancy with which Americans have struggled with the notion of taking off time from work . . . Americans engaged in a love/hate battle with their vacations — both wanting to take them and fearing the consequences. Relaxing did not come easily to American men and women who continued to use their leisure in the performance of various sorts of work — religious work, intellectual work, therapeutic work. Leisure and labor remained complicated and troubling categories. (Yardley 1999, 2)

In the Workplace

The fallout from the achievement ethic pervades every corner of the American workplace. The most visible impact is probably with respect to the kind of behavior that is rewarded on the job, what it is that gets a person promoted.

Results

In most businesses and offices it is the high achievers, sometimes also known as the "best performers," who advance. In other words, the bottom line in most workplaces is results. In the private sector in particular, many employees have quarterly or semi-annual goals, targets, or quotas they must meet. If they meet their target, they get to keep their job. If they exceed it, they get a bonus. If they exceed it by more than anyone else, they get promoted. It may be true that results are not the only measure of an employee's worth in America, but they are certainly the single most important criterion for advancement.

Promotion based on results helps explain one of the most common criticisms made about managers in the United States: that they have no "people" skills. This is no doubt in part because the skill set it takes to achieve — being aggressive, competitive, impatient, and driven — is in many ways quite different from the skill set it takes to motivate and support others to achieve. The qualities that get people promoted into the management ranks, in short, aren't necessarily the ones they'll need after they get there. So unless they already happen to have those other qualities — and haven't suppressed them too completely in the relentless pursuit of their targets — then they'll only accidentally be good managers. One can't help thinking there wouldn't be quite so many books published every year on leadership in the United States if leading people came a bit more naturally to those at the top.

The United States is not unique in rewarding achievement, of course; high achievers are valued and rewarded in almost all cultures, especially in the business world, and quotas or targets are likewise not peculiar to the American workplace. What *is* different is the somewhat single-minded emphasis on achievement in America, the degree to which performance beats out all other criteria as a measure of an employee's value to the organization.

In one survey conducted by Charles Hampden-Turner and Fons Trompenaars, people from a number of countries were asked the following question: "Should an employee with a record of 15 years satisfactory performance with a company be dismissed because his current performance is unsatisfactory, or should his whole record and the company's responsibility be considered?" (1993, 241). Of the eleven countries in the survey, more Americans than any other nationality (57 percent) said that current performance alone should be the deciding factor. The percentages who gave that answer in selected other countries are presented below (241):

Canada	54%		Italy	28%
UK	43%		France	26%
Netherlands	38%		Sweden	25%
Japan	33%		Singapore	22%
Germany	31%			

"We want results," Americans are fond of saying, "not excuses."

In recent years it has become increasingly common in the private sector in America to dismiss older employees with considerable experience and accumulated wisdom but whose results have started to decline. Whether or not experience and wisdom are weighed in making these decisions, they obviously count for less than performance. To many non-Americans, this tendency to undervalue such things as dedication, commitment, accumulated wisdom and experience, and loyalty makes Americans seem uncaring and even ruthless. Needless to say, any foreigners who are expecting these virtues to be admired and rewarded by their American colleagues may be disappointed.

The value placed on achievements and results, with its implicit bias in favor of ends over means, may also explain the great lengths to which managers and others are sometimes willing to go in tolerating the behavior of difficult employees. Someone who might be fired, or at least disciplined, in other cultures — an eccentric, perhaps, or someone who is very difficult to get along with or even insubordinate — might be forgiven these lapses in America if he or she is also a top performer, or, as Americans might put it, as long as he or she "delivers" (i.e., gets results). A European expatriate working in the United States for a large American multinational company recounted the story of this company's "most famous" employee, a man in sales who dressed entirely in black, wore a silver chain where everyone else wore a tie, and had a ring on every finger. This man, "who would have been kicked out in Europe," somehow had a way of connecting with customers and was eventually made vice president of sales for the company's largest product line.

Efficiency and Quick Results

The achievement ethic also helps explain the American obsession with efficiency and with anything that contributes to or supports being efficient. If getting things done is a good thing, then getting more things done — faster, cheaper, and with fewer people — is an even better thing. The efficiency ethos contributes to a number of other workplace behaviors, such as the need on occasion to go around the chain of command (which is forgiven, if it works — i.e., if it gets results — but resented if it doesn't) and the direct style of communication (whatever else it may be, being direct is certainly efficient). To some extent the efficiency ethic even contributes to the notorious American obsession with anything that's new; new, after all, is almost always improved, and improved by definition works better and is therefore more efficient.

To some extent the achievement value also explains the "short-termism" Americans are often accused of, their famous impatience for results. If self-respect and the respect of others come in large part from one's achievements, then there is a certain built-in pressure to see those achievements sooner rather than later. Americans don't like to wait very long for results, in short, because there is so much at stake. This may be one reason most American companies issue quarterly earnings reports, suggesting that three months is already a long time to wait for results. Compare this with German companies, for example, who "are not preoccupied with immediate results," according to Edward T. Hall. "It is important for Germans to complete action chains and so they find it inconvenient and disruptive to be asked for quarterly financial statements and reports; instead, they provide annual financial reports. [This] slow pace is hard on Americans" (1990, 37).

The desire to see results quickly is partly responsible for the general lack of enthusiasm Americans have for long-term projects or for any work that has a somewhat delayed payoff. "Americans not only want to *do* something," Lynn Payer has written in her book *Medicine and Culture,* "they want to do it *fast,* and if they cannot, they often become frustrated" (1989, 137). Americans are impatient, get bored easily, and by and large do not have much staying power. The drive to achieve, it turns out, is also the drive to achieve quickly.

This pressure to achieve, and especially to achieve quickly, is made all the more intense by the frequency with which people in the United States change jobs over the course of their working life — an average of eight times for the typical American. As soon as you take a new job, the pressure to achieve, to prove yourself in the new position, starts all over again.

Is it any wonder that Americans are too intense for many non-Americans? They are so focused on results and achievements — so competitive, driven, and ambitious — they use up all the oxygen in the room and leave everyone else gasping. They're very charged up, come on strong, and tend to run over anything in their path. You don't really talk to Americans or work with them; you just get out of their way.

The value placed on speed also helps explain the somewhat conflicted American attitude toward quality. The fact is that quality takes time — and Americans don't like to wait. While American companies talk a great deal about quality, they are willing to sacrifice it if it means beating the competition to the market or otherwise improving the bottom line. Or they will release a product that is not perfect, that is "good enough," and work out the kinks in the new and improved second version. The Japanese and Germans, by contrast, will spend as long as it takes developing, testing, tweaking, and retesting a product, and only release it when there's no way to make it better. If the competition beats them to the market, they're confident that superior quality will eventually win out.

In their book *Working for the Japanese: Inside Mazda's American Auto Plant,* Joseph Fucini and Suzy Fucini note that

> [t]he American manager, having been raised in a bottom-line environment, tended to look primarily or even exclusively at end results when assessing a plant's performance. How many cars was the plant producing a month? What was the defect rate? As long as he received satisfactory answers to these questions, the American manager considered the plant a success. . . . The goal . . . was to keep cars rolling off the assembly line with no interruptions. Changes, even those that could improve the production process, were regarded as inherently disruptive and therefore undesirable. (1990, 32, 33)

The "good enough" mentality also means that Americans are not particularly thorough or overly worried about details, about "dotting the i's" and "crossing the t's." These things take time, and in the end they usually don't have much of an impact on the bottom line. "The perfect," Americans are fond of saying, "is the enemy of the good." And in most cases "good" is good enough for Americans.

All three cultures — German, Japanese, American — claim to be champions of quality; it's all a matter of degree. For German and Japanese manufacturers, quality is very close to the greatest good; for Americans, it has to compete with a number of other good things.

Planning and Teamwork

Another consequence of the achievement ethos is American impatience with planning. Somehow, preparing to do is just not as satisfying as doing. While Americans recognize that planning is essential to achieving, and may even admit that it is a *kind* of doing, it doesn't have quite the same cachet as an actual, measurable achievement. So it is that Americans tend to be somewhat restless and disengaged during the early stages of a project, when the foundation for action is being carefully laid, and become much happier and enthusiastic as the time to execute draws near. Americans would much rather act on a hastily designed plan and pick up the pieces as necessary than wait while the plan is being perfected.

A *Newsweek* article on the Daimler Chrysler merger highlighted the differing German/American attitudes on precisely this cultural phenomenon as one of the major sticking points between the two partners. "Americans favor fast-paced trial-and-error experimentation," the article observed, "[while] Germans lay painstaking plans and implement them precisely. 'The Americans think the Germans are stubborn militarists, and the Germans think the Americans are totally chaotic,' says Edith Meissner, an executive at the Sindelfingen plant. To foster compromise, Americans are encouraged to make more specific plans, and Germans are urged to begin experimenting more quickly" (McGinn and Theil 1999, 51, 52).

The focus on achievement also explains in part why Americans generally don't like to work in teams. The esteem and respect that come with achievements require being able to easily identify the people responsible for those achievements. But when one works on a team, it's inherently difficult to determine who is responsible and should get the credit for any particular result. While it's no doubt satisfying to be part of a successful team, one that has impressive results, it's not quite as satisfying as getting individual recognition.

Needless to say, the competitive streak in many Americans likewise makes it difficult for them to be good at teamwork or even to be interested in it. The essence of teamwork, after all, is cooperation, and many Americans would rather spend the considerable time and energy it takes to cooperate with others to pursue individual results. (Teamwork is examined in more depth in chapter 6.)

The achievement ethic also influences the American attitude toward risk. One of the reasons Americans are willing to take risks is because of the reward that lies on the other side, the success and acclaim that come with achievement. In a culture where the means receive far less scrutiny than the ends, taking risks is easily forgiven. The other, almost irresistible appeal of risk in achievement-oriented cultures is the fact that while you can often get the same results without taking the risks, you won't get them nearly as quickly. Delayed results are still results, of course, but for Americans the wait can be excruciating.

Achievements You Can See

Taken to its extreme — and Americans tend to be an all-or-nothing kind of people — the achievement ethos leads to the belief that whatever cannot be quantified cannot be truly valued. Most Americans know better, of course, but it must be said that by and large the most satisfying achievements for Americans are those that are tangible, measurable, and visible — in other words, easily recognized by others. This may explain why many Americans are not particularly attracted to the service sector, especially to the so-called helping professions. Tangible results are just not the norm in many service sector jobs, and they can also take a long time coming. If they are even seen at all, the consequences of having "touched someone's life" or "given someone hope" or "made someone feel better about himself or herself" may not be apparent until years later.

Americans are deeply conflicted about the service sector. It is important, essential work that has to be done, and Americans greatly admire people who choose to do it, but it's not the sector one chooses if one is ambitious or wants to be well remunerated. A recent survey of college students found that only 40 percent were even considering going into government service, with most citing the "bureaucratic" and "inflexible" nature of the work environment and the inability to "go high" as their reasons for lack of interest. They were turned off, apparently, by the perceived limits on what they could accomplish and especially on how much they could accomplish. They wanted jobs with potential, in other words — the potential to achieve.

Their great fondness for doing tends to make Americans suspicious of most forms of not doing, especially talking and thinking. Their attitude toward talk, not all talk but talk that comes at the expense of doing, is made clear in a number of common expressions: "He's all talk and no action," "Talk is cheap," "Put your money where your mouth is," "Watch what we do, not what we say," "She talks a good line," and "Cut to the chase." In practical terms this wariness toward talk translates into such things as a general dislike for meetings (especially ones that are poorly run), a tendency to distrust people who are a bit too articulate ("smooth talkers"), and a general disinclination to act on the basis of talk alone but to wait and see if the person actually "delivers" on what he or she has promised.

Americans also tend to undervalue what we might call the achievements of the mind, things like ideas, analysis, theories, and paradigms. By and large Americans aren't interested in these things for their own sake, although they can become interested if they are shown what they can do with an idea or how they can apply a theory. In the same way, Americans don't particularly value the activities that produce these questionable outputs, things like research, study, reflection, and vigorous discussion, activities that at best only indirectly result in achievements. This is at least part of the reason Americans put down what they call academia, because many believe that the people in academia don't actually do anything; they just talk and think.

How Americans See Others

Americans sometimes regard people who are not sufficiently achievement-oriented as being lazy and unmotivated. They may come across as having very little drive or ambition, as not caring very much about whether they succeed, and as not worried enough about the bottom line. They may even come across as blasé or lacking in self-respect.

Similarly, if people are not willing to work nights or even an occasional Saturday (at least at the manager and middle manager level) or not willing to schedule their vacation around important milestones or due dates at work — if they let personal or family considerations unduly influence their work life — then they may come across to Americans as not "caring enough," meaning they are not very dedicated or committed to their work.

When people spend too long on tasks that don't contribute directly to results — too much discussion, analysis, or planning — they may come across to Americans as obsessed with details, excessively cautious, or very indecisive. By the same token, when people worry too much about taking risks, when they want to delay a roll-out or a product launch, for example, to do more testing or have another focus group, they strike Americans as timid and needlessly thorough.

Quick Tips:
Advice for Working with Americans

- Clear away obstructions that keep people from getting things done, such as elaborate procedures, a long chain of command (multiple sign-offs), or excessive testing.
- Quick decisions are almost as good as the right ones; planning, analysis, and discussion are necessary — up to a point (and Americans may reach that point before you will).
- Never act complacent or satisfied; you can always do better.
- Don't micromanage your employees; let their achievements be their own.
- It doesn't have to be perfect; "good enough" is good enough for Americans.
- It's okay to be aggressive; in the end you will be judged more by your results (the bottom line) than your personality.
- Don't be surprised if Americans expect you to work late or on weekends.

6
On Your Own

Americans don't like to depend on other people. They don't like to owe them, need them, or be beholden to them. They are generally quite wary of entanglements, of being encumbered, of anything that limits their ability to be true to themselves. In a word, they want to be free — and freedom in the United States boils down to not having to worry about what other people think or what they will say; it means having to answer to no one but yourself. If that sounds like a prescription for loneliness, which it does to many people, Americans would shrug their shoulders and say it's simply the price one has to pay to be independent. American laws, not surprisingly, are conspicuously weighted in favor of protecting individual rights, very often at the expense of society.

This does not mean that Americans don't like to help other people or even to be helped by them. Everyone needs a hand on occasion, and Americans are very quick to offer support and encouragement, often going out of their way to help relative strangers, people they may never see again. Nor does it mean that Americans never join groups or belong to civic, fraternal, or social organizations; there are thousands of such organizations, with millions of members happily working side by side for some cause greater than themselves. Individualism American-style doesn't mean not caring about others; it means not giving up control of one's life and one's destiny to others, being able to make one's own decisions as free as possible from outside influence.

In one of the most extensive studies of individualism (and its opposite, collectivism) in the workplace, Geert Hofstede administered a questionnaire to the employees of IBM in 66 countries. From participant answers, Hofstede then ranked the countries from most individualist to least (or most collectivist), according to the following general definitions:

> *Individualism* pertains to societies in which the ties between individuals are loose; everyone is expected to look after himself or herself and his or her immediate family.
>
> *Collectivism* pertains to societies in which people from birth onwards are integrated into strong, cohesive groups, which throughout people's lifetime continue to protect them in exchange for unquestioning loyalty. (1991, 51)

The United States ranked number one, the most individualist of all societies.

It's no accident that the cowboy was for so long the most popular icon of American culture, for the cowboy is the personification of the self-reliant individualist. He lives beyond the effective reach of society and has no ties — no house, no possessions, no family or friends (though he is *very* fond of his horse) — nothing that circumscribes or otherwise limits his freedom. He interacts with society (the community) by choice, always on his own terms, and only for short periods, moving on, significantly, whenever other people start to expect things from him. As psychologists would put it, cowboys have "commitment issues."

It should be noted that while cowboy virtues may appeal to individualist, self-reliant Americans, they're not nearly as attractive to the rest of the world. In many ways the cowboy stereotype personifies precisely what rubs most non-Americans the wrong way about people from the United States. Cowboys tend to be blunt, undisciplined, and reckless. They "shoot from the hip," for example, saying whatever they think to whomever they please and letting the consequences be damned. They have a take-it-or-leave-it attitude, aren't interested in compromise, and "ride roughshod" over objections, complaints, or opposition. They're rough and uncivilized, lacking in manners, social skills, and polish. The cowboy may indeed personify much that is American about America, but that's not always a good thing.

In the Workplace

Individualism, American Style

Individualism shows up in a number of subtle and not-so-subtle ways in the workplace. One of the most common is the typical American's desire to be left alone to do his or her job. Americans hate to be micromanaged, to have the boss — or anyone else — watching over them, telling them what to do. A good boss gives subordinates plenty of room and lets them approach him or her if they need something. This doesn't mean Americans don't take orders or follow instructions; it means, rather, that once someone makes a request or gives instructions, one should leave the person alone to carry out the request in whatever way he or she feels best. In the workplace at least, Americans generally don't mind being told what to do — they know this is a manager's responsibility — but they do mind being told how they should do it. The best managers issue their instructions and then disappear back into their offices. (For more on the manager/subordinate relationship, see chapter 9.)

Individualism is also a great support for the American habit of being direct. If people rely mainly on themselves, there's no reason to hold back, to not tell others what they think or describe things the way they are. "The value orientation of individualism," it has been noted,

> propels North Americans to speak their minds freely through direct verbal expression. Individualistic values foster the norms of honesty and openness. Honesty and openness are achieved through the use of precise, straightforward language. . . . (Gudykunst and Ting-Toomey 1988, 102)

Another form individualism takes on the job is the attitude of the average American toward working on a team. As discussed in chapter 5, Americans don't like to work on teams, and they aren't very good at it.

They don't have the right instincts for cooperating and no real knack for consulting or collaborating. Teamwork, after all, means subsuming the will of the individual to the needs of the group, the letting go of a certain amount of control and autonomy, and this does not come easily to Americans. To need, and especially to have to depend on others, goes against the grain for people who place such a high value on being independent.

It is telling in this context that whereas behaving as a team is the default workplace mode in many cultures — the instinctive, natural manner of interacting with colleagues — Americans typically only turn to teams as a last resort, when *their* default mode, individuals working more or less on their own, isn't up to the task. It cannot be coincidental that Edward Deming, the father of total quality management — a highly team-based approach to quality — got nowhere with his ideas when he tried them out with General Motors but was very successful when he took them to Japan.

This may explain why Americans are obsessed with teamwork and team building, why it's a regular offering of the training division and gets so much attention in management and organizational development circles; teamwork has to be actively stressed, encouraged, and supported — has to be trained into people — precisely because it does not come naturally to most American workers. One suspects that if the need to develop better teams was not consistently kept at such a high profile, it would have no profile at all.

Even when they do turn to teams (after all else has failed), the American idea of a "team" is quite different from that of truly team-oriented cultures, such as those in the Asia-Pacific region. Indeed, the kind of teamwork that occurs in Asian teams is so subtle, unconscious, and effortless that it is rarely even noticed by Americans and other Westerners, much less practiced. In many of these more collectivist, group-oriented societies, individualism is an alien concept; in one Chinese dialect, in fact, which has no word for *individualism,* the closest synonym is "selfishness." For workers from such cultures to see themselves and to perform as part of a team is instinctive and automatic; no special effort is required, for example, to suppress personal ambition for the good of the group, to keep personal opinions to oneself for the sake of group harmony, or to sacrifice individual well-being or personal comfort in a spirit of cooperation. Only if they had to work more independently would these workers then struggle and perhaps even need "individual building" training.

Another reason Americans may not be good at teamwork is their strong desire for individual recognition. They like to be singled out personally and given credit for their achievements — many companies and businesses select an employee of the month or an employee of the year — but this is not easy when those achievements are the handiwork of a team.

Charles Hampden-Turner and Fons Trompenaars asked respondents in twelve countries which type of job they preferred:

A. Jobs in which no one is singled out for personal honor but in which everyone works together.
B. Jobs in which personal initiatives are encouraged and individual initiatives are achieved.

Ninety-seven percent of Americans picked *B*, compared, for example, with the Japanese or the Singaporeans, of whom only 49 percent and 39 percent, respectively, chose *B*. In *McDonald's* restaurants in Asia, management selects the crew of the month, an approach that is unlikely to catch on any time soon in the United States (1993, 57).

Live and Let Live

Another consequence of valuing individualism is the tendency it has to make Americans a very tolerant lot. If everyone is going to be so strongly encouraged to be himself or herself, to become his or her "own person," as Americans like to say, then other people can't very well object to the person one decides to become. In the workplace this means Americans tend to tolerate a wide range of work habits — also known, tellingly, as "personal styles" — many of which would be considered disruptive or unprofessional in some countries, all in the name of individual rights and self-expression.

Thus you will find Americans bending over backward to indulge all manner of idiosyncrasies, quirks, peccadilloes, and oddball behavior among their colleagues. "That's just so-and-so's style," they'll say, or "He's just doing his thing." In recent years there have been numerous lawsuits when companies have tried to regulate such things as dress or personal appearance. For this reason American managers may come across to some non-Americans as overly indulgent and permissive, and American workers as spoiled and unprofessional.

It naturally follows that Americans are extremely reluctant to judge other people. If everyone is authentic, just being who she or he has to be, then there's no basis for judging another person. Who is one person, after all, to say that another person is not being himself or herself? Even more important — non-Americans, take note — Americans do not like to *be* judged (except, of course, on their performance, which is always fair game). This may be one reason Americans find it so difficult to fire workers and why they would much rather just lay them off; that way, there's no judgment involved.

Individualism also explains in part the American attitude toward rules and regulations. The point of most regulations, after all, is to restrict or otherwise control behavior, and Americans instinctively chafe at anything that appears to limit their individual freedom. They prefer, therefore, to err on the side of fewer regulations, even if that creates uncertainty and ambiguity (some would say chaos) in the workplace.

Loyalty

The independent streak in Americans also affects another workplace issue: the question of employee loyalty. For the most part, Americans do not feel a strong allegiance to their employer, and the feeling is mutual. Employees and employers have a largely opportunistic relationship, each looking out primarily for his or her own best interests. Just as workers feel no obligation to stay on with a company when it no longer serves their interests, neither do companies feel obliged to retain employees when it no longer serves the company's interests. While there may be more mutual loyalty in smaller companies, in general the employee-employer bond is not strong in the United States.

"Organisations exist independently of their members," John Mole has written of American business.

> The needs of individuals are seen as subsidiary to the needs of the organisation. Each member has a well-defined function to carry out and if that particular function no longer has any part to play, then neither does the person doing it. The readiness of companies to fire surplus or under-performing employees and the corresponding readiness of employees to change companies in order to further a career are part of an arm's length relationship between individuals and an organisation. . . . [This] is accepted as the way things work. (2003, 262)

Employees *are* expected to be dedicated and committed to their companies while they still work there, however.

How Americans See Others

In general, individualistic Americans regard people from more collectivist cultures as timid, conformist, not willing to stand up for themselves, and overly concerned about what other people think. They're too deferential, not aggressive enough, don't insist on their rights, and spend too much time worrying about and trying to get a consensus before acting. They seem to lack confidence and not to care enough about whether they get credit for their achievements.

Non-American bosses who don't give their American subordinates the considerable independence they expect will come across as micromanagers who meddle and interfere and don't trust the people who work for them. To Americans this kind of boss stifles creativity and ingenuity, is overbearing and insecure, and in general "needs to let go," meaning have a bit more faith in his or her employees.

For their part, hands-off American bosses may feel that non-American subordinates need too much direction and guidance, aren't independent enough, and are afraid to take any responsibility. Such people are considered "high maintenance," meaning they need a lot of attention and support, and may also be seen as lacking in self-confidence and initiative.

Americans who shy away from making personal judgments and are used to a wider range of work styles being accommodated on the job may find managers from other cultures strict, rigid, or intolerant. They get involved in things that aren't their business, such as what employees wear or how neat they keep their offices or cubicles, and they suppress individual expression and originality.

Quick Tips:
Advice for Working with Americans

- As a boss, sketch out the big picture and then let subordinates "do their own thing"; give instructions and guidance — and then disappear.
- Americans prefer individual recognition and like to stand out.
- Try to keep rules, regulations, and detailed procedures to a minimum; it makes Americans feel "penned in."
- If you want Americans to work on teams, give them plenty of coaching and plenty of time to get used to it; their instinct is to compete, not collaborate.
- Don't expect corporate loyalty from American workers.
- Don't interpret being challenged as a sign of disrespect.

7
Time Matters

[T]ravelers from abroad have invariably recorded and still record today the same impression: Why this American impatience? Where was and is the fire? What is the deadline each American is trying to beat?

— Luigi Barzini, *The Europeans*

One of the first things most non-Americans notice about Americans is that they never seem to have enough time and are always in a hurry. As the saying goes, "They want everything yesterday." No matter what they are doing, a certain urgency pervades the behavior of Americans, both on and off the job. "The American obsession with time is not limited to the business sector," one observer has noted. "They do *everything* in a hurry, even things they enjoy. Writer Calvin Trillin has noted that when traveling, Americans 'drive long distances as if they were being chased'" (Engel 1997, 58).

Take note of some of the chapter titles in a book called *Time Tactics of Very Successful People* (Griessman 1994):

- The Myth of "Free" Time

- Find Hidden Time

- Become a Speed Learner

- Learn to Focus

- Make the Most of Downtime and In-Between Time

- Learn to Recognize and Avoid Time Thieves

- Enlist Others to Save You Time

- Master the Art of Interrupting

Are you feeling anxious yet? Good. You're supposed to.

While several factors come together to form the American attitude toward time, surely one of the greatest influences is the achievement ethos described earlier. Given the great emphasis on achieving in American culture and the inextricable link between achieving and/or making money and time, it's no wonder time is such a precious commodity. From the American perspective, only two things can truly limit achievement — time and effort — and while people have a certain amount of control over how much effort they make, they have none over how much time they have. If they are in a hurry, it is primarily to cram more effort — hence more achievement — into an amount of time that is distressingly finite. As might be expected of a people who have learned to control and dominate so much else, the inability to conquer time is especially galling to Americans, and they're working very hard on the problem, with legions of scientists vigorously probing the secrets of aging.

Another reason Americans may feel so stressed about time is that in at least one sense they actually have less of it than people in some other cultures. The day isn't any longer in these other places than it is in the United States, but it can seem to be because the inhabitants of these countries don't have to divide their time among as many people as Americans do. I have briefly discussed universalist and particularist cultures in chapter 4. Particularists (who tend also to be collectivists) divide the world between ingroup and outgroup. Toward the members of their ingroup — immediate family, extended family, and close, lifelong friends — individuals owe complete allegiance and are bound by a series of responsibilities and obligations, which are mutual and reciprocated. Toward their outgroup — the rest of humanity — particularists recognize no obligations or responsibilities (they have their own ingroup to look after them). In particularist cultures, only people from one's ingroup have a claim on one's time, and while that claim can be considerable and even onerous on occasion, they are obliged only to divide their time among a finite number of individuals. Indeed, in particularist cultures, such as many of the countries in the Middle East and Latin America, it is very difficult to get an audience with someone unless you are from that person's ingroup, or more commonly, can at least claim an indirect link, such as being a friend of an ingroup member. In these cultures, not surprisingly, almost everything is done through "connections."

Universalists (who also tend to be more individualist) typically don't even use the ingroup/outgroup vocabulary. While they make distinctions between family, close friends, acquaintances, and strangers, recognizing different degrees of closeness and responsibility, there is no such thing as an outgroup, that great mass of humanity toward whom one has no ties of any kind. To put it another way, universalists, such as Americans, divide the world into people toward whom they have specific and binding obligations and those toward whom they have general and loose obligations. But there isn't anyone toward whom they have no obligations. In universalist societies, while some people may have a greater claim on one's time than others, everyone has at least a potential claim, and that can make the day go by very fast. It also explains why the people from more particularist cultures sometimes find Americans impatient, unrealistic (about how long things can take), reckless (doing things too quickly), and brusque (dispensing with pleasantries to "get down to business").

Meanwhile, until they learn how to beat or at least make more time, Americans work very hard at the next best thing — saving time — which is to say, doing more in the same amount of time. One way to accomplish this, of course, is simply to do everything faster, especially activities such as eating or shopping, which don't count as an actual accomplishment; hence the popularity of fast-food and drive-thrus of every description (including, in Las Vegas, drive-thru weddings). Another way to make more time is to do more than one thing at once, such as talking on the phone, dictating memos, or eating breakfast in one's car (it has been estimated that 25 percent of Americans do so), writing e-mails on the commuter train, or engaging in the ubiquitous breakfast meeting and working lunch.

In the Workplace

Obsession with Efficiency

In the workplace, the urge to save time explains in large part the great American obsession with being efficient. Anything that increases efficiency is taken very seriously in America, just as anything that undermines it is to be avoided or eliminated. Being well-organized, for example, is a quality highly prized in the workplace, mainly because people who are organized don't waste time, theirs or anyone else's. Prioritizing is another highly valued practice, for it too recognizes that time is limited and there is a corresponding need to rank activities in order of importance.

Making schedules and sticking to them are two other hallmarks of efficiency, two practices that not only make one more efficient but also allow others to be. Schedules are extremely comforting and reassuring to Americans, and for a very good reason: they create the illusion that people *can* actually control time. A schedule, after all, is a way of pre-assigning a certain amount of time to a certain accomplishment, suggesting that it is the scheduler who ultimately has the upper hand. The scheduler does not, of course — witness the panic that sets in when people are late for an appointment or when things take longer than planned — but it is important to indulge the illusion and pretend that schedules keep time in its place. It makes Americans feel better.

Brian Tracy, author of *The 100 Absolutely Unbreakable Laws of Business Success* quoted earlier, feels quite strongly about this aspect of time. "A positive mental attitude," he writes,

> . . . increases your energy, your creativity, and your capacity to get greater results. And a positive mental attitude is rooted in your feeling that you have a "sense of control" over your life. This sense of control is the key issue in peak performance. When you have too much to do and too little time, you can start to feel overwhelmed. . . . Time management is the tool that you can use to control the sequence of events and thereby take complete control of your life. (2000, 280)

In the workplace, the need to stay on schedule has many consequences. You should always be on time for an appointment or a meeting — especially for a meeting, where many other people's time is also at stake. Being late is one of the worst sins in the workplace, not only because it wastes time but also because it threatens to expose the entire fiction that people can somehow dominate time.

You should also keep very close track of your time and not allow the appointment or meeting to exceed its scheduled length. This is one of the main reasons Americans want a meeting to have an agenda, because an agenda is a kind of schedule, a way of keeping track of whether or not the meeting is unfolding in a timely manner. One of the reasons Americans tend to dislike meetings is because a meeting means turning control of one's time over to someone else, someone who may not take very good care of it. It's bad enough to waste's one's own time, but it's even worse if someone else wastes it. If it appears that a meeting or appointment you are conducting is going to take longer than planned, you should always offer to end it on schedule and arrange to continue later. If people don't mind going over the scheduled time, that's fine, but you should ask their permission.

Their love of schedules also means that Americans don't like to be interrupted. An interruption, by definition, is unplanned and unexpected and is therefore bound to put pressure on a person's schedule. Americans acknowledge this by apologizing whenever they "drop by" another person's office unannounced or by asking "Is this a good time?" when they telephone someone. There is in fact a hierarchy of "interruptability" in the American workplace, based, not surprisingly, on how valuable a person's time is perceived to be. The higher up a person is in an organization, the less likely he or she is to be interrupted, usually only for emergencies (or to speak with someone even higher up).

In a world where sticking to a schedule is so important, changing a schedule can be tricky. At a minimum, a change of schedule should never be last minute; you should always notify the other party or parties as far in advance as possible. This does depend somewhat on your rank or position, however; the higher up you are in an organization, the more important your time is perceived to be and the more acceptable it is to have to cancel or change your appointments. But even then, you should acknowledge the seriousness of the situation by making an apology or at least offering an explanation.

What is true for schedules is also true for deadlines. Americans are very precise about due dates; they are not flexible on this topic and do not regard deadlines as in any way approximate or best guesses. If you're not able to meet a deadline for some reason, you should let Americans know immediately; they may not be very happy — it means adjusting the schedule, after all — but that is nothing compared to the unhappiness they feel if they find out at the last minute. Generally, the further a deadline is in the future, the easier it is to negotiate a change.

Americans flock to classes on time management, where they are taught to keep track of how they use their time and techniques for using it better. One technique they learn is to use e-mail whenever possible instead of the telephone, mainly because in the e-mail mode one is in control of his or her time, whereas on the telephone another person is involved. (Some time-management experts even advise deliberately calling other people when you know they're not in so you can leave a message on their voice mail and not have to talk to them.) Even in e-mail mode, Americans are taught to be extremely selective about who they copy on their messages and to always fill in the "subject" box, so that time-deprived recipients can quickly decide if they actually need to open the message.

Getting to the Point

Concern about time also explains why Americans like to "get down to business," as they say, why they usually keep greetings and small talk to a minimum and proceed almost at once to the matter at hand. It also explains the American fondness for quickly getting to the point in a conversation, and especially for not getting off the subject, particularly at a meeting where the time wasted while someone "beats around the bush" or "goes off on a tangent" has to be multiplied by the number of attendees.

Americans are likewise very impatient with lengthy background explanations when someone is making a presentation, often jumping in to ask the speaker to "cut to the chase." When *they* give presentations (see pages 158–60), Americans usually start with their main points — key findings, results, conclusions — and provide the details later if there is time.

The emphasis on quickly getting to the point in a conversation or a meeting, their seeming impatience with context and details, can sometimes leave the impression that Americans aren't very thorough or curious, that they aren't interested in or capable of grasping the nuances or subtleties of the matter under discussion. They seem to want to understand just enough to be able to act. The related habit of wanting to simplify complex matters, stripping them down to a few basics or "talking points," only adds to their reputation for not being very "deep," that they can't be trusted to understand anything that is too complicated or intricate.

Quicker Is Better

Americans' preoccupation with time (and the pressure to achieve and make money, which lies behind it) makes them restless and impatient. People who derive a large measure of their respect and self-esteem from their accomplishments naturally want to see those accomplishments sooner rather than later. Accordingly, they have a short-term mentality; they don't like to wait, they hate delays, and they expect immediate results. A week can be a long time, and a month can be an eternity. This explains in part why Americans are always changing what they do or the way they do something; when they don't see results almost at once, they feel great pressure to try another approach. It may also help explain why Americans aren't afraid of improvising if the situation calls for it; whatever its limitations and risks, improvising is always faster than the alternative.

Americans want quick decisions and immediate responses — what they call "fast turnaround" — and are impatient with anything that slows down the pace of action, such as too much analysis or deliberation, too many procedures or regulations, too many layers of management, or having to build a consensus before making a decision. "Try to avoid analysis paralysis," Andy Bruce and Ken Langdon write. "Many decisions are based on less than perfect information. Avoid waiting for more information if it means you will decide or take action too late. Time is money . . ." (2001, 17).

This demand for quick decisions leads many to conclude that Americans must be quite reckless; after all, if that's how *they* make important decisions, that can only mean they don't spend very long worrying about the consequences. In the end, the desire for everything to happen fast is more evidence for the widespread belief among many non-Americans that for all their talk Americans are not really interested in quality.

Time pressure also contributes to the "good enough" mentality many Americans have — the attitude that things don't have to be done perfectly or the best they can be but simply good enough to please the customer or client. Perfection takes time, and when the choice is between doing more things and doing fewer things perfectly, many Americans will choose the former. "The perfect solution produced late," it has been noted, "is a free gift to the competition" (Bruce and Langdon, 35). Americans struggle with this issue, however, because they also profess to be very concerned about quality. In the end they get around this dilemma by defining quality in a way that enables them to have their cake (doing everything fast) and eating it too (doing things well).

"Many of the projects or tasks that you have to do are a lot like running hurdles," notes time-management guru B. Eugene Griessman:

> You aren't supposed to knock over the hurdles, but there's no bonus for clearing them by an extra margin either. All you really have to do is get over them. . . . The best hurdlers clear the hurdles, but just barely.
>
> This advice seems to discount the value of high-quality work. That's not true. In most instances quality is what the customer wants. . . . Your customer may not want you to spend a great deal of time on . . . a project but may want you to do all parts adequately. The trick is to find out what is really wanted by the customer. (94, 95)

The "trick" in the United States anyway.

How Americans See Others

People for whom the clock is always ticking aren't especially forgiving of those with a more relaxed attitude toward time. People who treat schedules and deadlines more casually — for example, those who understand that interruptions or delays can't always be helped, that life is sometimes shockingly oblivious to what's written down in a daily planner — frustrate and deeply annoy Americans. They aren't serious about their work or about business; they are unprofessional, unorganized, and inefficient; they are unreliable and can't be trusted, and they have no motivation.

Americans also think people with a relaxed attitude toward time spend too many hours socializing and trying to get to know each other. They aren't that interested in getting things done, and they don't care nearly enough about the bottom line. And while they probably don't mean to be, they are also insensitive and rude because they waste other people's time.

People who don't get to the point quickly in a conversation or a meeting, who get off the subject, or who present too much background information and too many details are seen as unfocused, unorganized, and rambling. They don't think clearly; they lose sight of the big picture; they complicate things needlessly; and they're not very decisive.

Because they equate the efficient use of time with being able to accomplish more, Americans find people who are casual about time as not being very ambitious; while they may not actually be lazy (although one wonders at times), they're certainly not very dedicated or committed.

People who are thorough, deliberate, and careful in making decisions, who try to anticipate and think through the consequences of their actions, come across as overly cautious and even timid to Americans. They see such people as obsessed with details, paralyzed by too much analysis, or far too consultative. They're not being careful, they're just afraid to act.

People who are willing to wait longer to see results, who believe some things don't happen quickly and cannot be rushed, may come across to

Americans as passive, fatalistic, or even lazy. They need to be more aggressive and more proactive; if they really cared about their product or their business, they would *do* something.

Quick Tips:
Advice for Working with Americans

- Be on time for appointments and meetings, so you don't waste other people's time or throw them off their schedule.
- Conduct meetings and appointments efficiently so they end on schedule.
- Respect deadlines; if you're not going to meet a deadline, let others know as soon as possible.
- Get to the point quickly in a conversation, meeting, or presentation.
- Keep it simple: in a presentation, just give the basics. Put details in a handout or later in an e-mail.
- In a meeting, don't ramble, talk off the subject, or get bogged down in details — and don't let others do this.
- Be decisive; Americans expect a fast turnaround. *Any* action is better than inaction.
- Don't spend very long "getting to know Americans"; they will expect you to quickly get down to business.
- Don't be offended. They think they're being considerate by respecting your time.

8

Communication, American Style

Every country has its own way of saying things. The important point is that which lies behind *people's words.*

— Freya Stark, *The Journey's Echo*

The noted interculturalist Edward T. Hall has said that culture *is* communication. What he meant is not so much that culture and communication are one and the same, but that since so much of behavior involves communication of one kind or another — and since culture is such a fundamental influence on all behavior — it's difficult to say where one stops and the other begins.

Workplace behavior is a case in point. One way or another almost everything that happens in the workplace involves some kind of communication, the sending or receiving of messages. Whether it's face to face, over the telephone, or via e-mail, whether it's written, verbal, or nonverbal, whether it's one-on-one or in groups, most work gets done through the exchange of various kinds of information. To the extent that culture influences how people send and interpret messages, to work effectively with people from another culture you have to understand its communication style. If you don't understand the messages Americans are sending and if they don't understand the messages you're sending, how can you expect anything you do together to be very successful?

Communication is a very big piece of the cross-cultural puzzle — and it is also the piece about which it is the most difficult to make any useful generalizations. Of all the behaviors humans engage in, surely communication is among the most context-driven; what people say and how they say it almost always depends on the situation or the circumstances. To generalize about communication, therefore, to make statements that by definition ignore the circumstances, is something of a fool's errand. The exceptions to almost any general cultural observation about communication start piling up even before you've finished making the observation. But while communication itself may defy categorization, it may be possible to generalize about communication *style,* and it is certainly possible to compare communication styles *across* cultures.

Straight Talk

It may not be possible to generalize about communication, but that hasn't stopped people from trying, and one of the most frequent observations made about Americans is that they are direct. "Direct" is in the eye of the beholder, of course — Americans don't seem particularly direct to each other, and especially not to people from even more direct cultures, such as the Germans, the Israelis, or the Dutch — but on balance Americans are *relatively* more direct than people in many other cultures. Consider, by way of evidence, all the expressions Americans have for how they like their conversations to go. They want people to get to the point, tell it like it is, face the facts, let the chips fall where they may, and put their cards on the table. And they don't like it when people mince their words, beat around the bush, pull their punches, or hold back. They like the unvarnished truth, plain speech, straight talk.

Straight talk is probably the best way to characterize American-style directness, but what exactly does it mean to talk straight? It's easier, in a way, to say what straight talk is *not;* by and large, straight talkers don't imply, hint, or intimate what they mean; nor, as the phrase itself suggests, do they go around or somehow sneak up on the topic. On the contrary, straight talkers make a beeline for the topic. Straight talk is generally thought to be spontaneous, natural, and uncontrived; it comes from the heart, not the head. Straight talk is the emotions speaking, as close to unfiltered feelings as you can get in speech. The often-heard expression, "*Say* what's on your mind," captures perfectly the essence of straight talk. "American speech is remarkably straightforward," Stephanie Faul has noted. "They tell it as it is, even when it's not a particularly good idea to do so. Linguistic subtlety, innuendo, and irony that other nations find delightful puzzle Americans, who take all statements at face value. . . ." (1999, 61).

This "literalness," or taking words at their face value, is another important feature of American-style directness. Americans have great faith in words, regarding them as the primary carrier of meaning, and they quite literally "take people at their word." They try very hard to match their words as closely as possible to their thoughts or feelings, so that what a person says is truly what he or she "means," that is, what he or she is actually thinking or feeling. In classic straight talk there should never be any need to have to *interpret* what a speaker means; speakers will *say* what they mean.

This is how Americans expect their words to be taken and also how they interpret the words of others. They do not expect listeners to read between the lines of what they say — in direct speech, there is nothing there — and they are notoriously inept at reading between the lines of what other people say. After all, people who go to great lengths to put what they mean *in* the lines, in the words they use, have no experience with having to look elsewhere for meaning, and they are not very good at it. Almost nothing bothers Americans more than people who say one thing and actually mean another — it's not only confusing, it's dishonest — and the practice has been enshrined in the decidedly pejorative expression of "speaking with a forked tongue."

The forked tongue approach, incidentally, is alive and well in the speech of some politicians, which probably explains why politics is one of the most reviled professions in America. Not only do politicians typically not speak from the heart, they don't even speak from the head, preferring, rather, to speak from the heads of other people, most notably those of their advisors, pollsters, and other political pulse takers. It was his refusal to ignore this political norm and insist on speaking plainly that got Harry Truman into so much trouble — with other politicians, that is; the masses loved him for it. Fittingly, *Plain-Speaking* was the title of his oral autobiography. We might note, in passing, how an especially egregious lapse from plain speech, egregious even for a politician, that is, got Bill Clinton into a pile of trouble ("It depends on what the meaning of *is* is.") and has already become one of the most famous moments of his presidency.

Finally, we have recent word from another seasoned politician, Al Gore, that failing to speak plainly is a mistake he will not repeat if he ever runs again for elective office:

> Former vice-president Al Gore conceded today that his 2000 presidential campaign was too heavily influenced by polls, consultants and tactical maneuvering, telling key supporters that if he runs in 2004, he will "let it rip" and "let the chips fall where they may."
>
> "If I had it to do over again . . . I would spend more time speaking from the heart. . . . To hell with the polls, tactics and all the rest." (*The Washington Post*, June 30, 2002, A4)

Even if they don't often practice it, politicians are smart enough to know that "letting it rip" and "speaking from the heart" are much admired by Americans. But enough about politicians. If we've gone on about them, it's not for the pleasure of dragging them through the mud but to illustrate how much Americans value unvarnished, unadorned, straight talk, honored in the breach in the case of some politicians rather than in the observance.

The Origins of Straight Talk

Many of the themes we have been tracking in these pages come together to create the American habit of speaking plainly, beginning with the ideal of egalitarianism. In a culture where people are believed to be inherently equal, there is no need — hence no tradition — of editing what one says to suit the rank or status of the listener vis-à-vis one's own. If all listeners are equal, then the only conversational imperative is to be honest, to choose words that most accurately convey what one thinks about the matter under discussion.

Americans are quite proud of the fact that they talk the same way to everyone. One of the worst mistakes you can make with Americans is to "talk down" to them, to talk to other people as if you are somehow superior to them. Similarly, Americans are very suspicious of and uncomfortable with anyone who appears to be "talking up" to them, speaking to them in a fawning, obsequious, or servile manner. This is so unnatural for most Americans that they tend to assume that anyone who behaves in this way has ulterior motives and is not sincere.

Self-reliance and individualism also go hand in hand with being direct. If you answer only to yourself, if you do not depend on the indulgence and sufferance of others for your success or well-being, then you can say what you think without fear of the consequences. In a sense, being direct is not simply a habit for Americans but practically a badge of honor; the right to say what you think, to anyone anytime, is the ultimate expression of individual liberty. The "self," after all, is supreme in individualistic societies, and self-expression, by extension, is therefore a fundamental right.

This doesn't mean that Americans are deliberately rude or uncivil, but they do instinctively chafe at any suggestion of having to muzzle their feelings or adjust their opinions to suit the occasion. When they err, they tend to err on the side of too much self-expression, not too little. "They believe in the end," as I have observed elsewhere, "that any unfortunate consequences of too much self-expression are still preferable to the consequences of excessive self-restraint" (Storti 2001, 37). As one 19th century English visitor noted, "Civility cannot be purchased from Americans on any terms. They seem to think it is incompatible with freedom."

Being direct is also efficient, and efficiency, as we've seen repeatedly, is high on the list of American values. The more direct someone is, the less chance there is of being misinterpreted or misunderstood, and misunderstandings are practically the pinnacle of inefficiency. Being direct also saves a lot of time, the time it would take to find out what the person really means.

American directness may also be a function of the fact that for many immigrants English was a foreign language. People who don't know a language very well, who are struggling merely to make themselves understood, do not have the luxury of choosing their words carefully or otherwise engaging in nuance or subtlety. They're obliged, rather, to use the few words and limited structures they know, and their speech can accordingly sound quite primitive.

High and Low Context

Ultimately, communication style comes down to what people in a particular culture see as the purpose of communication. For Americans, the primary purpose of communication is to exchange information, and being direct is surely the fastest, most efficient way to do that. But for many other cultures, information exchange is not the primary purpose of communication, and in these societies the need to be direct is neither understood nor appreciated. Nor, for that matter, is the communication style in these other cultures understood or appreciated by Americans. The differences between these two styles of communication, often referred to as "low context" and "high context," account for so much cross-cultural confusion and bad feeling — they are at the root of so much misunderstanding and so many cross-cultural incidents — that it behooves us to spend a few minutes on this topic.

The United States is what is considered a low-context culture, *context* meaning "the knowledge or experience one member of a group has in common with other members of that group," a measure, in short, of the degree to which the lives of group members are interconnected. In low-context societies, where people tend to have a more individualist as opposed to a more collectivist mentality, people live relatively independent lives, associating with others more as a matter of choice than of circumstances. Americans are not antisocial, but they do have a well-developed sense of privacy, guarding their own privacy and respecting that of others, and they tend to err on the side of leaving each other alone. Being by themselves (with one or two family members or close friends) is the natural or "default mode" for most Americans, requiring little or no effort; only if they want to be in the company of others do Americans have to exert themselves.

In leading such relatively independent, separate lives, Americans are not particularly knowledgeable about or attuned to what is happening in the lives of the people around them, including those with whom they have regular contact. They don't know what has happened to these people since they last saw them, what has changed in their lives, what decisions they've made, what they're concerned with or thinking about. The relative lack of shared knowledge Americans have about each other's lives makes the exchange of information the first order of business when people meet. Several expressions Americans often use at such moments make this function of conversation quite explicit, such as, "I've got to fill you in," "We've got to catch up," or "I need to get you up to speed (or bring you up to date) on this." Not surprisingly, it is content or substance — what we might call "raw information" — that is the priority in such conversations, while style or form, the manner of speaking, occupies a much lesser place. The style of these exchanges, in short, is decidedly stripped down and unadorned; in other words, it is our old friend straight talk.

"In a fluid, ever-shifting society of people who were mostly strangers to one another," the English writer Jonathan Raban has observed about American culture, "nothing was tacit, nothing could be assumed in the way of prior knowledge or experience. Everything had to be stated plainly and underlined. Irony was out" (*The Washington Post,* December 20, 2003, C4).

The American low-context mentality not only makes straight talk necessary, it also makes it quite acceptable. If people are not attuned to the inner lives of each other, not privy to each other's feelings, insecurities, fears, and doubts, then it can hardly be expected that they will take these things into account in conversation, choosing their words carefully, for example, so as not to hurt another person's feelings or cause them to lose face. If you cannot be expected to know another person's feelings, then how can you be criticized for hurting them? Americans are not deliberately insensitive, of course, but the fact is that ultimately they have much less to be sensitive *about* than people from some other cultures. In low-context societies, therefore, straight talk is not likely to cause much offense. And even if it does, the consequences of causing offense, of upsetting or embarrassing someone else, are necessarily less in individualist cultures, where people do not rely so much on each other for their survival or well-being.

Now compare, for a moment, life in high-context cultures, where the primary unit of survival is the group, not the individual, and where the well-being of the group takes precedence over — and ultimately guarantees — the survival of the individual. In such cultures, the lives of group members (usually extended families and a few close friends) are completely intertwined, and privacy is neither sought nor expected. Virtually everything that happens to one group member is known by the rest of the group; indeed, since the group spends so much time together, most of what happens to one member of the group happens to them all. The people who live in high-context cultures, in short, have a great deal of shared experience and typically don't need to exchange information when they get together; they are together so often, either physically or by other means, that they already know those things about each other's lives, which people in low-context cultures have to explain when they get together.

For high-context people, therefore, the purpose of conversation is not so much to exchange information — so much is already known or intuitively understood — but to strengthen and deepen personal bonds and relationships, to make the group that everyone depends on even more cohesive and unified. The greatest good in such cultures, the glue that keeps the group together, is harmony, and the greatest sin is to do or say anything that disturbs that harmony. "Filipinos grow up with ultra-sensitive feelers for hints of impending personal storms," Alfredo and Grace Roces write in their book on Philippine culture,

> feelers a Westerner does not have. At the faintest indication of conflict, someone within the group is always ready to bury the symptoms beneath the surface. Direct confrontation is frowned upon and regarded in the worst light. . . . Public conflict is taboo because someone is bound to lose face and this would lead to wider trouble. (1994, 8)

When people from such cultures speak, the primary goal is not to say anything that will upset another group member or somehow cause him or her to lose face, and the secondary goal is to send a message. Thus, people are very careful about what they say and even more careful about how they say it, especially when the message is not what the other person wants to hear. As the reader can imagine, the people in such cultures are almost never direct.

Nor do they ever have to be explicit, that is, to come out and say what they mean. The people in high-context cultures are so in tune with each other, so mutually aware, that they have to say very little in order to be understood. They can suggest, imply, or hint at what they mean, and that is usually enough. In many cases words are not necessary at all; the message comes in the form of what is *not* said — or, very often, in the form of nonverbal communication, which is relied on much more in such cultures.

Relatively Speaking

It's entirely possible that a lot of Americans will not recognize themselves in the previous pages. Some would even refute the characterization made of them as straight-talking truth seekers, citing all manner of situations where they regularly pull their punches, hold their tongues, and otherwise amend the naked truth for fear of causing offense. In a word, while other people tend to find Americans quite direct, they don't necessarily see themselves that way. Since non-Americans are quite likely to come across Americans who are in denial about their communication style, it's important to address the subject.

Actually, it's not very complicated; *most* people don't see themselves the way others see them (the phenomenon that makes books like these possible and necessary), and Americans aren't any exception. Most people see themselves from the inside, as it were, from the perspective of their own culture; theirs is an absolutist point of view rather than a relative or comparative one. Every culture, therefore, has an entire range of all types of individuals *as judged by the norms or standards of that culture.* So-called "indirect" cultures, therefore, like the Japanese, have their version of indirect, direct, and blunt communicators; so-called "direct" cultures, like the United States, likewise have indirect, direct, and blunt speakers. Americans *are* direct compared to the Japanese, and the Japanese *are* indirect compared to Americans, but not in any absolute sense. To put it all another way, it's entirely possible to be forthright and blunt in Japan, and likewise, it's entirely possible to be vague and subtle in the United States. It's all a matter of degree.

There are, incidentally, some countries where people are even more direct than Americans. Pride of place probably goes to Israel, followed closely by the Germans, the Dutch, and perhaps the Scandinavians. People from these cultures do not find Americans especially direct or abrupt and may even see them as insincere and vague; they perceive Americans, in short, the same way Americans perceive the Japanese or people from southeast Asia.

"Americans tend to think of themselves as very direct and to the point," Greg Nees has written.

> Compared with many cultures they are. Compared with Germans they are less so, although this depends on the situation and the particular speech act.... [I]n terms of stating facts, offering criticism, and issuing direct commands, Germans are generally more direct, leading to perceptions of them as opinionated, blunt, and brusque know-it-alls. (2000, 72)

In a fair fight, Israelis would normally win the straight-talking competition. They prefer the "direct, confrontational, no-frills style" of communication, Lucy Shahar and David Kurz have observed, a style they compare to sandpaper, which is similarly "rough, grating, and devoid of a smooth finish." Americans will frequently use the phrase, "I'm going to tell you the unvarnished truth" when they are about to communicate something painful.... But the American unvarnished truth is considerably smoother than Israeli truth delivered sandpaper style (1995, 78, 79).

With these caveats and qualifiers in mind, let's visit the workplace and see how these low-context Yanks actually communicate at the office.

In the Workplace

Directness on the Job

What forms does directness American-style assume on the job? The most common form is probably in how Americans state their opinions and in how they expect others to state theirs. If you ask them what they think about something — something you've proposed, something you've done, something you've heard about — by and large Americans feel obliged to give you "an honest answer," something that closely approximates what the speaker actually thinks or feels about the matter. The answer will be more or less honest depending on how well the two speakers know each other, and especially on the power relationship between them, but it will not usually be dishonest, that is, something *other* than what the person thinks.

This is true whether the opinion is favorable or unfavorable and whether or not he or she agrees or disagrees with you. The obligation to answer honestly is not somehow mitigated when the answer may not be what the other person wants to hear; indeed, plain-speaking Americans instinctively assume that what the other person wants to hear is "the truth," that is, what one honestly thinks or feels about the subject in question (also known, tellingly, as the "naked" truth). "Business discussions [in America] may be forthright to the point of being brusque," John Mole has observed. "Bluntness is preferred to subtlety. Some Europeans consider American openness as unseemly and brash, unaware that what they believe is their own sophisticated reserve may appear muddle-headed and devious" (2003, 264).

Listen to the advice on communication Stephen Viscusi gives to new American workers in his book *On The Job: How To Make It in the Real World of Work:*

> It's vital that your style of communication doesn't trip you up, that it doesn't create unnecessary problems. So you want to avoid ambiguity and indirect communication, because those qualities are the causes of so many problems. Instead, you want clarity and directness. That's what virtually everyone else wants too, because they allow the organization to function smoothly. (2001, 163)

The insistence on giving honest answers also explains another dimension of American directness: the relative ease with which Americans say "No." Compared to many cultures, Americans find it relatively easy to give a negative reply, to turn down a request, for example, or say they didn't understand something, that they're not available, that something is not possible or not convenient. For Americans, *no* is like any other answer; if it's the truth, then it's what they have to say. They may surround *no* with nicer words to make it go down better, but generally they won't change *no* to another answer in order to please the listener.

"Reluctance to emphatically state a negative response," Dean Engel has written,

> and the tendency to resort to euphemism ("That would be difficult") — common approaches in Asian cultures — are sources of aggravation to Americans, who are more concerned with knowing the intent of others than with having their feelings spared. Indeed, even at the cost of what others would consider good manners, Americans pride themselves on *saying what they mean* — in cowboy parlance, *shooting from the hip* — and they expect others to do likewise. (1997, 74)

Negative Feedback

All of the above notwithstanding, Americans struggle with giving negative feedback (though they have no trouble at all giving the positive kind). While this doesn't seem to square with their being direct, Americans draw the line when it comes to anything that could be seen as personal criticism or comments that might hurt another person's feelings. Whether it's because they want to be liked or to protect their own feelings, Americans are careful not to be too critical whenever someone asks for direct feedback about their performance. "Too critical" is in the eye (or ear) of the beholder, of course, but generally it consists of saying something negative without preceding it with something positive or without somehow qualifying the negative observation.

If you have done a very poor job on a report, for example, Americans will not simply say you have done a very poor job and leave it at that; they will say, rather, that the report is "pretty good" or "not bad" and then talk about how it "might need some work." It's called "damning with faint praise," and it is an exception to the "telling it like it is" style that Americans usually prefer. "A number of German acquaintances have told me they don't really feel comfortable dealing with Americans," Richard Lord writes, because they "tend to be altogether more circumspect in their criticisms, that they will pad the truth to protect the other persons' feelings" (1996, 50). (For more on feedback, see Giving Feedback, page 168.)

Cutting to the Chase

Another form American directness takes is the tendency Americans have to get to the point as soon as possible in a conversation. They tend to be linear in their thinking, looking for and taking the shortest distance between the starting point of an observation and the conclusion or end point. Thus they typically provide a minimum of detail or context in their statements and tend not to qualify their observations or otherwise clutter up the message with interesting but ultimately extraneous information. Accordingly, they get very impatient with digressions or other conversational enhancements that don't have a direct, immediate bearing on the point. They don't like it when speakers "get off the subject," "talk in circles," or otherwise fail to "cut to the chase." Ultimately, of course, all this is driven by the "real" point, which is: What are we going to *do* about the matter?

With their impatience for details and their desire to quickly get to the point, Americans strike many non-Americans as simplistic and naïve, in the sense that some things are not as simple, not as black and white as Americans want to make them. The "point," in other words, can sometimes be multifaceted and complex and only make sense when put in its proper context. By and large, Americans aren't very good at handling complex matters, at being able to examine something from several perspectives at once, for example, or accommodating conflicting ideas about an issue or proposal. They like neat categories and typically try to strip the complex down to a few basics, believing, as they often say, that "nothing can be that complicated."

While most Americans would probably not regard quickly getting to the point as being abrupt or direct — they would think it's just being efficient — it is often seen that way by people who prefer to slowly close in on their main point, all the while gauging the other person's reaction as the message starts to emerge and retreating or changing the subject if the reaction does not appear to be favorable. By getting right to the point, Americans don't give listeners time to signal their reactions or the speaker the chance to back off, thus setting up potential unpleasantness if the point is going to be contentious, for example, or embarrassing to the listener.

In a related habit, Americans waste little time in what they call "getting down to business" in a conversation, preferring to dispense with greetings and small talk as quickly as possible and get to the point of the meeting, which for low-context Americans is primarily to accomplish some kind of task. But for high-context people, for whom the object of a meeting or conversation is primarily to cultivate and strengthen the personal relationship (and secondarily to execute the task), dispensing with the pleasantries is not only rude, it's missing the point. This helps explain why Americans strike some non-Americans as being interested only in the task and not in people, which in turn gets them branded as opportunists, focusing exclusively on the deal or the sale. Not surprisingly, such people can never be entirely trusted.

At a Meeting

Another characteristic of straight talk is that it is usually not adjusted to suit the situation. In many cultures, what people say in public, at a meeting, for example, is quite different from what they say one-on-one in private. In public you say what you have to; in private you say what you think. But Americans tend to talk equally straight whether they're speaking in front of several people or to just one other person. They may choose their words more carefully in a meeting, but the public and private versions of what they say will closely resemble each other. Americans generally think of meetings as being inefficient anyway (see Meetings, page 155), so meetings where people don't say what they think are an even greater waste of time. Even at the risk of causing minor offense or embarrassing someone (already a lesser risk in the United States than in other cultures), Americans give honest answers in meetings — and expect them from others. Indeed, if you approach an American after a meeting to tell the person what you really think, he or she will probably ask you why you didn't say so in the meeting.

It is also acceptable to disagree with someone at a meeting. While in some high-context cultures people prefer to confine disagreements to one-on-one encounters and may even use third parties to convey the message — to avoid confrontation and to allow all parties to save face — Americans often disagree with each other in public. They like to "get to the bottom of things," as they say, "get everything out in the open," and "find out where everyone stands" on the matter being discussed. They believe it is important to ask questions, raise objections, and express opposing points of view at a meeting; indeed, this is the purpose of many meetings. And if this sometimes means disagreeing with other people, then so be it. There are important exceptions, of course; typically, Americans would be somewhat careful about disagreeing with their boss or more senior persons at a meeting, and they would not as a rule disagree with their boss in front of outsiders. Nor would they disagree with a guest at a meeting, someone from outside the division or the organization.

Confrontation

At the same time, and somewhat improbably, Americans generally don't like arguments or confrontation. They believe that it is entirely possible to disagree with someone without getting into an argument, which they define as getting agitated or upset and being on the verge of losing self-control. They believe this because they also feel that people ought to be able to separate themselves, hence their feelings and self-image, from the issue being discussed, to confine the conversation to the facts, the problem, the situation, without, as they say, "pointing the finger" at anyone. It ought to be possible, in short, to disagree with or take exception to something another person has said or done without getting upset, attacking the individual, or otherwise "getting personal." If you have to get personal, then you have, as Americans say, "gone too far."

   Americans are especially wary of arguing with friends and close colleagues (who are often one and the same). In spite of their habit of being frank, Americans very much want to be liked, and arguments can easily end up with people not liking each other. "American friends try to offer positive support to each other," it has been noted,

   and to establish harmony. If they disagree, they may down play their differences, agree to disagree, or try to smooth things over to maintain good relations. Bickering, argument and open disagreement are signs that people are not getting along well and that the relationship may be in danger of falling apart. (Asselin and Mastron 2001, 89)

Direct Questions and Requests

Just as they are direct in their answers, Americans also tend to be direct in their questions — in the sense that with only a few exceptions, Americans feel free to ask about whatever is on their mind. In a culture where saving face isn't very important, where people are mainly interested in knowing the truth, very few questions are out of bounds. If it's not particularly embarrassing or shameful to have to admit to mistakes or personal shortcomings, to reveal problems, or to tell people things they may not want to hear, then there's no reason to worry about questions that might evoke such responses. There can be only delicate questions, in short, in cultures where there are delicate answers, and in low-context cultures, the delicacy threshold is relatively low.

Americans are also direct in the way they make requests; if they need or want something or want you to do something, they will simply ask. If you have or can do that thing, you will answer yes; if you don't have or can't do that thing, you will answer no. This is so completely natural to Americans that they find it hard to imagine there could be any other way to handle requests and, therefore, that their own approach could possibly come across as direct.

In high-context societies, however, making requests is a potentially delicate matter, in the sense that if the person of whom the request is made has to turn down or refuse it, then he or she is put in the awkward position of upsetting or disappointing the questioner. For this reason, people from more indirect cultures rarely make direct requests, unless they already know the answer will be yes; rather, they simply describe what it is they need and leave it at that. Other indirect speakers will hear this description for what it is (a call for help) and either answer in the affirmative, if they can do what is being "asked" of them, or say nothing at all if they cannot. Either way, since a request is never actually made, it never has to be refused. Needless to say, this tactic will break down completely if it is used on Americans; since they don't interpret a statement of need as a request, they don't reply to such statements. But indirect speakers should not interpret the American failure to reply as a negative answer.

Indirectness: A Primer

As the above example amply illustrates, one of the most important things for non-Americans to understand about low-context/straight-talking Americans is that by and large they do not understand people who don't talk straight. If one is a direct communicator, surrounded by other direct communicators, then one has very little experience with, hence very little understanding of, indirect communicators. If you are from a more high-context/indirect culture, such as much of the Asia-Pacific region, Latin America, and much of Africa, you should realize that Americans will not recognize many of the most common techniques you will use, to say nothing of the messages you're trying to convey. This section offers a few observations on how techniques for communicating indirectly are perceived by Americans (although we note, for the record, that these techniques would not seem indirect to those of you who actually use them but only to more direct speakers).

Understatement

The first thing indirect communicators must remember is that Americans will interpret what you say literally, which means that above all you should be very careful about using any kind of understatement. The essence of understatement is to say less than what you actually mean, knowing your listener will supply the rest by "reading into" your words the real message. But Americans expect people to *say* what they mean and only understand as much as is actually said.

If you remark, for example, that doing something may be "a little difficult" or that you have "a small suggestion," meaning that doing that thing will be impossible and that the "small suggestion" is a polite request, Americans will not understand. Taking your words at face value, they will assume "a little difficult" means entirely possible if slightly inconvenient, and that "a small suggestion" is nothing to worry about. If you want Americans to know something is not possible, you have to use the words *not* and *possible* in close proximity, and if you're making a request, don't call it a suggestion, especially not a small one.

Bad News

People from indirect cultures rely especially heavily on understatement whenever the message to be communicated is somehow awkward, delicate, or embarrassing. If you have any kind of negative feedback to give, for example, or any kind of bad news — We're behind schedule, We need help, There's a problem, This is going to cost more or take longer than we thought — or if you have made a mistake or don't understand something, indirectness is called for. Because all of these exchanges potentially involve loss of face, whether the speaker's or the listener's, the message has to be phrased very carefully, so carefully that the delicate matter is often not explicitly mentioned at all.

Negative feedback, for example, often takes the form of faint praise, saying someone is doing an "adequate" job, that something is "okay," that the work is "acceptable," or even saying nothing when feedback is requested or clearly expected. The same goes for delivering bad news: if there's a big problem, you may call it a minor difficulty or a slight setback. If you're an Indian subcontractor, let's say, running behind schedule on a project, you will try to convey this to an American with typical understatement — such as asking if this is still a good schedule, by saying how very busy you are these days, or by saying that *almost* everything will be ready on the due date. If you use these methods to say you're not going to make the deadline, the American will not understand.

You will also need to be more direct in asking for help. Americans won't realize you need help if all you do is say how complicated what you're working on has become or if you talk about the last time the American helped you. These might be obvious calls for help in your culture, but Americans won't read anything into these statements; they'll just interpret them literally and be quite puzzled.

You should remember that just as Americans do not usually understand understatement, neither do they use it. If an American says something will be a little difficult or that someone's work is acceptable, that's exactly what he or she means, nothing more and nothing less. As a rule, there's no need to read anything into what an American says, to supply what is missing or deliberately left unsaid. When Americans speak, nothing is missing, and chances are very good that anything that has not been said has not been thought.

Saying No

Since negative answers can be awkward or delicate, indirect speakers have worked out ways of saying no without ever having to actually use the word. The problem for Americans is that they take you at your word, so that if you don't say the word *no,* an American doesn't hear no. If, as an indirect communicator, you use any of these techniques with Americans, they usually don't work, with the inevitable result that you're quite sure you have said no and the American has simply not heard it.

One common way indirect speakers say no is to simply avoid the question they have been asked. If it's not polite (or necessary) to say no in your culture and you are in a position when you can't say yes (because it would be untruthful), then you would typically give a negative answer in one of two ways: by saying nothing at all or by sending the question back to the person who asked it. But you should remember that while other indirect speakers will know what you mean by sending the question back or by avoiding it all together (i.e., no), Americans will simply be confused. When you say nothing in response to a proposal or suggestion, Americans usually take that as a positive sign, not a negative one, and when you ask Americans a question (even if it is their own question coming back to them), they treat it like any other inquiry and simply answer it.

Consider the following exchange:

BILL: We need to schedule the next team meeting.

HIROKO: Good idea.

BILL: How about next Tuesday morning?

HIROKO: Tuesday?

BILL: Yes, would 10:30 be OK?

HIROKO:	10:30? Is it good for you?
BILL:	Yes, it's fine.
HIROKO:	I see.

If you're Hiroko in this exchange, you've made it quite clear that this meeting time is not good for you. First, you refused to answer Bill's question and sent it back to him ("Tuesday?"); then you did the same thing with the question about the meeting time ("10:30?"); then you asked him a question about his own question ("Is it good for you?"); and finally, you never said *yes*. For you, these are very direct ways of answering in the negative. But here again you should remember that Americans like Bill will interpret what you say literally; questions will be interpreted as questions (not polite forms of no) and will be answered; and never saying yes just means you never said yes, not that you meant no.

A variation on this same technique is to comment in the negative about a proposal or suggestion by asking the speaker what *he* or *she* thinks of it instead of saying what you think of it yourself. What you mean when you do this is something like, "I'm not commenting on this because if I did, I would have to say something negative." But this is not what an American will think. Such an exchange might go something like this:

LINDA:	Hi, Carmen. How are you?
CARMEN:	Fine, and you?
LINDA:	I'm OK. I was wondering, Carmen, what would you think if we decided to move up the deadline for the new software release?
CARMEN:	Move it up?
LINDA:	Just by a week, at the most.
CARMEN:	Do you think it's possible?
LINDA:	Should be. But what do *you* think?
CARMEN:	You don't see any real problems, then?

> LINDA: Not really. My people can be ready if your team can get it done by then.

Carmen doesn't like the suggestion, and she communicates this by immediately asking questions and also by never saying anything positive. But this is not how Linda will interpret this conversation.

Finally, many indirect speakers actually say no by using the word *yes*, followed by *but* or *and*, by some kind of qualification, additional information, or even a question, which is the "real" answer. The problem here, of course, is that Americans take your yes for your real answer and don't even listen to what comes next. Such a conversation might go like this:

> CAROL: How's the design coming along, Yang?
>
> YANG: Fine, fine.
>
> CAROL: Are we still on schedule?
>
> YANG: Oh yes. We're working extra hard on this.
>
> CAROL: Great. My people are anxious to see the new layout.
>
> YANG: Of course. When are they expecting to see it?
>
> CAROL: By the end of the week, like we agreed.
>
> YANG: I see.

If you're Yang, you probably think you've made it clear that you're not going to be ready by the end of the week. First you said you were "working extra hard on this," by which you meant you're behind schedule, and then you pointedly asked Carol when her people were expecting to see the design. Since you know the schedule, you know when her people are expecting to see the design; so what you obviously meant was that her people may need to adjust their expectations! But Carol will not read between the lines in this way; she will just take your words at face value — especially when you answer "Oh yes" to her question about being on schedule.

The thread that runs through many of these techniques is that in the case of a negative or disappointing answer, the message often comes in the form of what is *not* said, whether it's not answering the question or simply never saying yes. If you're an indirect communicator, then you know how to listen for what is not said, but Americans take people at their word — and if there are no words, then there is no message.

Exceptions to Straight Talk

Even Americans don't always peddle the unvarnished truth, and in fact they have several habits that tend to undermine their straight-talking credentials, beginning with their insistence on always looking on the bright side. Americans will go to almost any lengths to avoid sounding negative, pessimistic, or defeatist, even if it means being somewhat less than honest and candid. They try to stay away from topics they refer to as "downers" and to stay out of conversations that "bring you down," as in down from the giddy heights of optimism and happiness. These topics include anything to do with evil or the dark side of human nature, which Americans either ignore or try to explain away, anything that suggests failure, defeat, or any kind of setback — especially with death, the ultimate setback — or anything to do with limits or limitations, such as reasons why something cannot be done, should not be tried, or is not possible.

"The American language," Stephanie Faul has observed,

> embraces the bias towards good feelings. No one has a failure; he or she has a "deficiency rating." Someone doesn't have a near brush with death; he or she has a "life affirming experience." Stocks that plummet to half their value are not losers; they're "non-performers." Applicants who do not receive a job offer are "selected out." An upbeat business vernacular calls every problem a "challenge" and every massive layoff "right-sizing."
>
> All this mindless good nature . . . is enough to give a European a de-enhanced attitude. (1999, 63)

When they can't avoid these unpleasant realities, Americans try to trivialize them, either through language or by minimizing their significance.

Thus things are never as bad as they seem, never as hard as they look, will never take as long as you think, and are ever and always bound to get better.

Fantastic!

Another related characteristic that tarnishes the image of the straight-talking American is the national tendency to exaggerate. Americans see no particular value in describing something as it is if there's any way to make it sound better, and they routinely make highly inflated claims for their products, services, and abilities, for how fast or how cheaply they can do something, or how beautiful, strong, or long-lasting they can make something. Superlatives permeate the vernacular. Americans never settle for "good" when they can use "great"; what is great immediately becomes "fantastic"; and the truly fantastic is either "sensational" or "fabulous."

The American writer Bill Bryson, who lived for many years in England, describes how the same product has "to be sold in entirely different ways" in the United States and England:

> An advertisement in Britain for a cold relief capsule, for instance, would promise no more than that it might make you feel a little better. You would still have a red nose and be in your pajamas, but you would be smiling again, if wanly. A commercial for the selfsame product in America, however, would guarantee total, instantaneous relief. A person on the American side of the Atlantic who took this miracle compound would not only throw off his pj's and get back to work at once, he would feel better than he had for years and finish the day having the time of his life at a bowling alley. (1999, 11)

To some foreign observers, especially northern Europeans, the "feel good" rhetoric and the instinct to exaggerate seem to call into question the American commitment to straight talk. How can a people who pride themselves on telling it like it is refuse to see things the way they are? Part of the answer, suggested earlier, is that in the United States, as in any society, there are conflicting cultural influences; thus the instinct to tell it like it is may on occasion clash with the instinct to be positive and optimistic, and normally straight-talking Americans suddenly end up pulling their punches. People who are direct, in short, will not *always* be direct. Also, while Americans are rather good at *telling* it like it is, they're not nearly as good at *seeing* it like it is.

Political Correctness

Sooner or later the conversation about straight-talking Americans always comes around to the topic of political correctness. Numerous non-American observers have charged that thanks to political correctness Americans who might once have been free to say what they thought are no longer allowed to. Plain speech, it is said, has been replaced with politically correct speech, and double-talk has become the new national norm.

There is in fact some truth to this observation. At its core, political correctness is the American obsession with equality taken to an impractical extreme. If everyone is truly equal, then making distinctions between people is ultimately arbitrary and subjective, a random selection of one type — white people, men, thin women, very intelligent people — to serve as the standard against which others can then be measured (and, the implication is, found wanting). In a world where everyone is truly equal, it would not be possible to compare but only to describe, which is precisely what political correctness is all about. Hence, there are not disabled people but people who are differently abled, not fat and thin people but people who are differently sized.

If it's not possible to compare, then it's also not possible to judge, which is another of the central tenets of political correctness. Things can be understood only in their proper context, and all judgments, therefore, are automatically suspect and most likely biased. Everything is relative; one person's performance or attitude is not better than another person's; it is simply "different." There are no absolutes and, ultimately, no standards.

Politically correct speech is most important when it comes to discussing sensitive social matters: anything to do with race, gender, religion, ethnicity, sexual orientation, and any kind of physical or mental disability. Even for Americans, conversations about these topics have become linguistic minefields; every observation is so carefully qualified, every conclusion so highly tentative, and the use of euphemism so rampant that it is no wonder the American reputation for straight talk has taken such a hit in recent years.

Unless you're very experienced, you would be wise as a non-American to stay away from these sensitive topics. If you have to venture into politically correct territory, then observe very closely the expressions Americans use.

How Americans See Others

The relative subtlety of indirect speech means that many Americans misinterpret much of what high-context, indirect communicators say. Whether it's understatement, the meaning of what is *not* said, the ways of saying no, or the use of questions to disagree — these and all the other techniques described above are generally not used and not understood by Americans. The problem in these cases, of course, is that Americans think they *have* understood the indirect communicator, so that when it turns out they have not — when it turns out they have misinterpreted that person — Americans quite naturally assume they have been misled or even lied to.

These scenarios can take myriad forms, of course, depending on the particular message that was misunderstood and the particular inaccurate expectation that was thereby set in motion. One common category is the unpleasantness that ensues when a direct American explains something to a person from a more indirect culture, asks that person if he or she has understood, the person says yes, and the American believes that's the end of it. But the yes didn't mean the person had understood, the American doesn't realize that further explanation or clarification is needed (and doesn't offer any), and the job is either not done at all (as the person politely waited for additional instruction) or, just as common, is done incorrectly because the person simply tried something and hoped it was right.

Another common category is the bad news scenario. In these cases, indirect communicators have told direct types that they are falling behind on something, won't be able to meet a particular deadline, or could use some help; but they communicated this message with such delicate understatement — "We're putting every available person on this." "This is certainly a big job, isn't it?" "Do we still have the same deadline on this?" — that the plain-speaking American completely missed it. When the inevitable reckoning comes, the American is shocked to learn that the Indian vendor (for example) is behind schedule on the new software application, and the Indian vendor can't imagine how the American didn't know that.

A third, closely related scenario occurs when an American believes an indirect communicator has agreed to something (because he or she said yes) when in fact the person has not agreed. What the indirect type did, of course, was to use the word *yes* and then proceed to give his or her answer to the request — which the American, having heard the other person say yes, either overlooked or regarded as mere details.

These scenarios can play out in various ways, but all have one thing in common: they end badly. Americans either go away thinking indirect types are lying to them or deliberately misleading them or that they're manipulative, that they "play games," as Americans put it, telling everyone what they want to hear, or telling one person one thing and another person something completely different. In other cases, Americans may feel that indirect speakers are hiding something or somehow "holding back," not saying all they know or how strongly they feel about the matter in question. Finally, indirect types can come across as servile or even sycophantic to Americans, trying to ingratiate themselves with or flatter other people in pursuit of their own interests.

Americans also find indirect communicators very inefficient. As they see it, when other people don't say what they mean, then they have to try to figure it out. But who has time for these "guessing games"? It's also annoying when indirect people beat around the bush and never seem to get to the point, when they go off on tangents, or when they provide all manner of extraneous detail that just seems to Americans to get in the way of the message. Moreover, when people seem to take "forever" to get down to business, spending a lot of time catching up on each other's personal and family news and generally strengthening the personal relationship, they may strike Americans as not being very task-oriented or not taking business seriously.

In closing we should remember that there's nothing deliberate or intentional about the misunderstandings described in this chapter; it's not as if people are to *blame* for their communication style or that they're *trying* to misinterpret each other. A certain amount of misinterpretation is almost inevitable whenever a person from one culture tries to figure out what someone from another culture means. But even if they're not deliberate, these misunderstandings can be very frustrating and can easily undermine relations in the workplace. The Quick Tips in the box may help you avoid some of the more common pitfalls.

Quick Tips:
Advice for Working with Americans

- Don't expect Americans to understand understatement; they will interpret what you say literally.
- Don't say yes unless you actually mean yes, unless you actually mean I approve, I agree, I accept, I understand.
- If you want to say no, you must use the word *no*.
- When Americans ask you if you have understood something, they will not be offended if you say no (but they *will* be upset if you say yes when you did not understand).
- If you use any of the following techniques to express disagreement to Americans, they will probably not understand:
  - ask a lot of questions
  - say nothing in response to a suggestion or proposal
  - answer a question with a question
  - change the subject
  - bring an agreed-upon subject up again for further discussion
- Remember: When you think you're being blunt or even rude, Americans will probably think you're just being direct. And when Americans think they're being direct, you will probably think they're being rude.

9

Of Bosses
and Subordinates

When [the best leaders] are finished with their work,
people say, "It happened naturally."

— Lao Tzu, *Tao Te Ching*

Everyone who works is either a boss or an underling, and most
people are both. Only the person at the very top is not a subordinate, and only those at the very bottom don't have people they
manage. The manager-subordinate relationship is perhaps the most fundamental dynamic in the workplace and part of the subtext of almost
everything that happens between people on the job. In some situations,
it plays a leading, obvious role; in others, it's only in the background. But
it is always there, directly and indirectly influencing events and shaping
behavior. Whether you manage or are managed by Americans, or even if
you are personally outside the chain of command but work with people
on the inside, understanding the mutual expectations and assumptions
of bosses and subordinates in the United States is essential for success. If
you don't understand how the manager/subordinate dynamic plays out
in the American workplace, you will probably feel like a geologist who
doesn't understand plate tectonics.

There are many bosses out there: good ones and bad ones, secure and
insecure ones, bosses with a light touch and bosses with a heavy hand.
And all kinds of subordinates: ones who do best when they're left alone,
ones who must never be left alone, and ones you wish you *could* leave
alone. Needless to say, no two subordinates interact with their bosses in
quite the same way, and vice versa, so the standard warning about generalizations is very much in effect in this chapter. Nevertheless, there does

seem to be a core of common American traits that define the manager-subordinate dynamic, and these will be the focus here.

Power

To start to understand how bosses and subordinates interact in America, we need to address the whole question of power. Americans are deeply conflicted about power: they crave it, but they are loathe to be caught craving it; they say power doesn't matter, but they envy and admire those who have it; those who have power say it's a curse and a burden but fight to the death to keep it and get more of it. Nor do Americans have any qualms about exercising power; they can be quite ruthless, in fact, especially when compared with managers from many Asian and northern European countries. The irony is that while American managers are probably more ambivalent about having power than managers in most other countries, they are also among the most likely to wield it.

"Power is one of the last dirty words," writes Rosabeth Moss Kanter, one of the leading management gurus in the United States. "It is easier to talk about money — and much easier to talk about sex — than it is to talk about power. People who have it deny it; people who want it do not want to appear to hunger for it; and people who engage in its machinations do so secretly" (1997, 135).

Why all this coyness? Why can't Americans be more up front about how they feel about power? The reason, in a nutshell, is that at its core the exercise of power involves inequality, and as we've already seen in these pages, inequality is a very sticky subject for Americans. In any workplace, in any undertaking in which people act together for a common purpose, someone has to give instructions and someone has to carry them out; some people have to be subordinate to the authority and will of other people. This is true in all cultures, of course; what is different is the degree to which people in various cultures are comfortable with the fact that some people must have more power and influence than others.

Americans are not especially comfortable with this fact because of the premium they place on egalitarianism. Not surprisingly, when circumstances oblige Americans to behave in an unequal manner, to act as if they are superior to other people — as a manager must on occasion — this behavior doesn't feel quite right. In many ways, the exercise of power obliges Americans to forswear one of their deepest cultural values.

"In egalitarian American culture," Gilles Asselin and Ruth Mastron have observed,

> [c]ompanies talk of the participative workplace where employees are empowered to control their own jobs and destinies. The idea of having power over someone, or, worse yet, being under someone's power, makes most Americans vaguely uncomfortable. . . . In France and other Latin cultures, power is acknowledged and spoken of openly. High-level people use their power freely, usually to their own advantage, and are respectfully deferred to by those they control. (2001, 200)

The exercise of authority also conflicts with another deeply held American value, individualism, and further complicates the manager-subordinate relationship. Simply stated, independent, self-reliant Americans don't like to be subordinate — to anyone — and generally resent being told what to do. No wonder *power* is such a dirty word.

Bosses, American Style

Their decidedly ambiguous attitude toward power explains the great awkwardness with which many Americans embrace the role of manager, and that same awkwardness pervades the American style of management. By and large, Americans don't like to manage — or to be managed — and much about the American workplace is set up precisely to keep the genie (i.e., power) in the bottle, set up, in short, so that workers never have to witness the ugly spectacle of bosses throwing their weight around. When a boss *does* have to throw his or her weight around, then something has gone terribly wrong. In the United States, the best managers are those who manage least.

Less Is More

One of the most common ways bosses avoid having to exercise authority is to give most of it away to their subordinates. Relative to many cultures, American bosses typically delegate a great deal of responsibility to those under them, empowering them to make their own decisions and trusting them to run their own show. By and large, bosses who do not delegate, the dreaded micromanagers, are not admired. Bosses further abdicate their power by encouraging employees to take initiative and by rewarding them when they do. Bosses always like to be kept informed, of course, to know in general (though usually not in particular) what's going on, but they don't feel they need to manage everything that's going on.

Delegating responsibility and encouraging employees to take initiative are of a piece with another bedrock theme of American culture: the habit of judging oneself and others by achievements. If employees are free to make decisions and solve problems without management interference, then any results they get are their own. By wielding their authority lightly, American managers not only avoid the charge of being autocratic, they also enable employees to freely pursue their single greatest source of satisfaction and self-respect: their achievements. This in turn not only boosts employee morale and performance, it also makes management look good; managers are judged by their achievements, too, don't forget, and foremost among those is the output of their employees.

"Build an empowered environment," Ken Langdon and Christina Osborne have observed, in what is standard American management advice,

> by encouraging your team members to be less dependent on you as their manager. By delegating responsibility to team members you increase their control over what is achieved [and] . . . the team members are then able to work on their own . . . using their initiative to solve any problems along the way. This will increase their effectiveness and save you time. Stress that you would prefer people to come to you with solutions rather than problems. (2001, 14)

Because bosses do tend to delegate, it's not necessary to always check with a boss before approaching his or her subordinate about a matter that has been delegated to that individual; and it is likewise acceptable in most cases for that person to give you a decision (especially a routine decision) without first checking with the boss. Bosses do like to be kept informed of any important decisions subordinates make, but if the matter in question has been delegated, they would not necessarily expect to be consulted about it.

The habit of delegating helps explain the characteristic American attitude toward making mistakes on the job. For the most part mistakes are expected — and forgiven. If bosses are going to delegate authority, then they can't very well complain when employees use it. Empowering people doesn't just mean empowering them to do well; it also means empowering them to screw up. Employees should learn from their mistakes, of course, and not repeat them, but they should not be intimidated out of making them. At the same time, when subordinates accept authority they have to accept the consequences. If they do make mistakes, they are expected to admit them and not try to shift the blame.

Listen to a Jordanian banker comparing his experiences working at Western banks and at Arab banks. "Autonomy at the [Western] bank was very strong," he notes,

> At the moment you join the bank they make you feel that you are important, that you are able to make decisions, that you should not fear making decisions . . . and if you make a mistake, but not serious, they try to help you. From the first moment they let you feel that you are a responsible person . . . who supposes to lead, not to be led. At Arab banks it is the other way around; you do not do anything without referring to the boss, even as a manager, even if you are senior. It is highly centralized, autonomy is very minimal and they [senior top-level management] do not give you the benefit of having confidence, and if you make a mistake, it is against you. (Hickson and Pugh 1995, 197)

Two other practices that keep the power genie in the bottle are the use of specific and very detailed job descriptions and the profusion of procedures manuals. Job descriptions that spell out everyone's duties and responsibilities at considerable length make it unnecessary for bosses to have to step in and tell people what to do. Similarly, if bosses aren't actually going to run the workplace, if it is in effect supposed to run itself, then some systems are needed to make this possible. Hence, the profusion of procedures and operations manuals that explain in great detail how things are supposed to be done.

Finally, most American bosses leave their doors open at all times so that in the unlikely event that they are actually *needed* for something, employees can have instant access. Indeed, so far as subordinates are concerned, this is the main job of a manager in the United States: to be available. While employees definitely expect and prefer "hands-off" management, they also want the option of "hands-on" whenever they need it.

Command and Control

That's how it's all supposed to work anyway — it's what all the management books say, and it's certainly how most subordinates hope it will work — but it's not always what happens. For every hands-off, empowering manager, there's a manager who can't quite get the hang of delegating, who wants to know everything that's going on, and who breaks into a sweat whenever he or she hears the word *initiative*. But how can this be? Didn't these people get the message — the message that says people do their best work when you leave them alone?

They probably did get the message, but the fact is that American culture sends its managers mixed messages, and some managers handle the inevitable confusion much better than others. The management and leadership books may indeed say to delegate and empower, but senior management and stockholders tend to be much more interested in the bottom line, in results (usually spelled "profits"). In the final analysis, everyone, including the boss, has to produce; in fact, the boss *in particular* has to produce and is held more accountable for the bottom line than anyone else.

Understandably, this makes some bosses jumpy. All other things being equal, they would probably be quite happy to manage with a light touch, staying out of the way and letting people get on with their jobs. But all other things are frequently not equal, and middle managers typically come under considerable pressure to cut costs, improve performance, meet ever-higher quotas (usually with fewer people), increase market share, and otherwise "grow the business." Some bosses handle this pressure quite well, probably because they have some first-rate sub-ordinates (see Subordinates, American Style, pages 136–39) and because *their* managers are very supportive; whatever the reason, these bosses manage to be hands-off and still get maximum performance, hence stellar results, out of their people.

But other managers, who either aren't so lucky in their workers or their bosses, aren't so sure of themselves, or may simply be "driven" — manage with a vengeance, keeping a tight rein on subordinates, making most of the decisions, and sweating most of the details. It has been called the "command and control" style of management, and it is probably at least as common in the American workplace as the hands-off style everyone claims they practice.

In truth most managers probably move back and forth between the hands-off and command and control styles, depending on the nature of the particular task or function in question and the employees who are being managed. Even the most empowering of managers have to take control from time to time, and the most autocratic bosses have to delegate some tasks. There is, in short, an inherent tension in being a good manager in the United States, the result, at least in part, of competing cultural values that cannot always be reconciled. "Exercise authority," Robert Heller writes in a typically schizophrenic piece of American management advice, "but not unnecessary force, to achieve desired results. Sharing authority helps develop people's own talents. . . . Look also for whole areas that can be delegated, but always retain overall control." (1998, 53)

Finding the right balance between giving up power and staying in control can be stressful, which is probably why managers are more prone to nervous breakdowns than those who work under them. But at least they get paid more.

Informality

Non-Americans may also be fooled into thinking Americans are more laid back about power than they really are by the air of informality that characterizes manager-subordinate relations. American managers typically cultivate a low profile, going out of their way to act like — and to insist on being treated as — just another member of the team. If the worst thing anyone can do in the United States is to act superior, then people who are in a superior position have to be especially careful to act humble, hence the practice of everyone calling everyone else by their first name, bosses leaving their doors open, and managers making their own coffee. When an American, Tom Glocer, took over the venerable British media group Reuters, he made a few very American changes. "I like seeing the people I work with," he explained.

> So I tore down a bunch of walls [and] asked that my management team do the same, and we put up glass. I wouldn't say it has the buzz of a newsroom or a trading floor, but it is not the mahogany panel, please-book-with-the-secretary before you come in [look]. It is, "Oh, I see you are in, can I show you what I am working on?" Which is more my style, I guess. (Goldsmith and Deogun 2003, B11)

Bosses *are* informal with their subordinates in the United States, but the meaning is not that everyone is equal; it is, rather, that bosses should wear their power lightly and not act as if they deserve special treatment or should be deferred to because of their elevated status. Bosses should be especially careful never to act as if they're "above" doing certain things, especially certain menial tasks. "I didn't see myself as a boss," observes Jack Welch, former CEO of General Electric, about one of his first management positions, "but as a peer. We didn't have any pomp and circumstance. . . . I think ideally that is how a company works. It becomes a place of ideas, not a place of position" (*The Wall Street Journal, Boss Talk,* 2002, 4).

The irony is that so long as a boss behaves as if he or she is just like everyone else, then that boss will in fact *get* special treatment and *be* deferred to. Subordinates are always on the lookout for signs that becoming a boss "has gone to [someone's] head" or that the person "has forgotten where he came from" (that is, down here with the rest of us). Don't worry though; bosses who momentarily forget where they came from will soon be reminded that they too "put their trousers on one leg at a time."

Confused? Don't be. It's really quite easy: to be a good boss in the United States, just remember never to act like a boss.

Managers, Not Experts

Unlike some cultures, bosses in the United States are not expected to be subject-matter or technical experts in the areas in which they work. While many managers are experts, having worked their way up through the ranks in a particular division, technical discipline, or product line, many bosses are hired primarily for their managerial expertise or their people skills. The head of finance may not know anything about finance, but he or she may have good leadership skills or be good at down-sizing or at reinvigorating a low-performing division. It's not uncommon, therefore, for bosses to know less about a particular subject or be less adept in a particular skill than the people who work under them. Nor is it embarrassing for a boss to be unable to answer technical questions or be unable to perform a common task.

"American managers do not necessarily have all the answers," two observers have noted,

> and their subordinates do not expect them to. Coaching and developing one's team are important management responsibilities, and most managers would have no problem admitting that a subordinate is better informed in a certain area. . . . Such an admission from a French top-level manager would be the equivalent of giving the order to drop the guillotine blade. . . . [French] subordinates expect [their managers] to know everything and to have all the answers. Confessing one's ignorance is usually perceived to be a sign of weakness. (Asselin and Mastron 2001, 219)

In a multi-country survey, the French management specialist Andre Laurent asked people whether or not they agreed with the following statement: "It is important for a manager to have at hand precise answers to most of the questions that subordinates may raise about their work." While two-thirds of the Italian and 53 percent of the French respondents agreed, less than 18 percent of the Americans did (Hampden-Turner and Trompenaars 1993, 357).

Decision Making

By and large, decision making is not a consultative nor an especially participatory process in the United States, certainly not when compared with Western Europe and much of the Asia-Pacific region. Managers may feel the need to get "input," as they call it, to solicit opinions and ideas, but they do not feel compelled to build a consensus for a decision or to involve subordinates in any substantive way in their deliberations. Consensus building takes time, for one thing, and Americans want and expect things to happen fast. "Americans may lose patience with the participative, committee cultures of some countries," John Mole has written. "They do not look for consensus, in the sense of collective responsibility for a decision jointly arrived at, but for wholehearted commitment to a course of action for which one person carries total responsibility" (2003, 263).

Nothing slows down the pace of work more than bosses who can't make decisions, which is why being decisive — by which Americans mean getting minimal input and acting quickly — is one of the principal criteria by which managers are judged in the United States. In some contexts, a quick decision is almost as good as the right one. In his introduction to *Boss Talk,* a series of interviews with top executives, leadership guru Tom Peters advises managers to just "get on with it" when it comes to making decisions. "Don't wobble. . . . [M]aking a decision and moving forward and seeing what happens, even if it's messy, is far better than endless debate . . ." (*The Wall Street Journal,* 2002, xii).

For the most part, decision making American style is also consistent with the less-is-more, empowering approach to management described above. If delegating means anything, it means delegating the authority to make one's own decisions, and this is a general norm in the workplace. Subordinates don't like to be "second-guessed," as they call it, to have their decisions questioned or reviewed by management, so long, of course, as the matter decided is within the employee's area of responsibility. At the same time, workers are expected to take full responsibility for the decisions they make.

The same holds true for bosses, who are also free to make their own decisions about the areas they are responsible for. Many of these decisions affect employees, of course, and while bosses are expected to consult employees about significant matters, they generally don't feel the need to build a consensus for their decisions. Just as managers are expected to trust the decisions subordinates make, so too subordinates are expected to trust bosses in the decisions they make.

Leadership

What is a manager's job, then, if it's not to supervise employees? Judging from all the books on the subject, a manager's primary job is to lead. While no one's quite sure what this means — the books breathlessly urge leading from the top, from the bottom, from out in front, from behind, from within — there is basic agreement on two main points: (1) a leader articulates the general direction of the office or division, its primary mission or role, and, perhaps most important, (2) a leader coaches and encourages his or her employees. "You need to engage people in where it is you're going in a serious way," Steve Ballmer of Microsoft explains about defining the direction, "and have them really feel it and be enthused by it. They need a mission" (*The Wall Street Journal, Boss Talk* 15).

While employees generally want to be left alone, they do appreciate and expect encouragement from the manager. They like to be told that they're doing a good job, to be praised for individual accomplishments, to be recognized for their contributions — and the more often the better. Americans in general are very free with praise, and managers are no exception. The other way managers encourage subordinates is by giving them all the support they need to do their work. Subordinates don't expect to be told how to do their jobs, but they do expect to be given the resources they need to perform, such as technology, training, administrative and logistical support, even some general guidance from above. Workers are ultimately judged by results, after all, by their output, and it's a manager's responsibility to his or her employees to provide them with the tools and the overall work environment they need to maximize their output.

In this context it should be noted that all that has been said about power notwithstanding, American subordinates actually do want their bosses to *have* power; they just don't want it used on them. They want their bosses to be respected and influential in the company or organization, and especially to have what is known as "clout," the ability to get the attention of senior management and persuade them to do their bidding.

Subordinates expect their bosses to look out for them and get the support that's needed for the division. The unspoken contract between boss and subordinate is something like this: I'll do my job (i.e., by myself, without help) and you'll do yours. Bosses should be seen but not heard around the office, perhaps, but they should be seen *and* heard everywhere else.

Relationship with Subordinates

Bosses must be very careful not to have favorites, to make exceptions for certain employees, for example, and not others, to be seen to protect or make excuses for certain people, or to judge different employees by different standards. Managers are only human, of course, and like all humans they have more in common or get along better with some people than with others, but they should never act that way in the workplace. Next to behaving as if they are superior, which is the worst thing a boss can do, treating certain employees better than others is the second worst. Playing favorites violates that most basic of American values, egalitarianism, and is one of the quickest ways to undermine morale and performance in the workplace.

Bosses usually keep their distance from the personal lives of their employees. While subordinates often befriend and socialize with each other (see Workplace Relationships, pages 146–48), it is much less common for a boss and one of his or her subordinates to become personal friends. If this does happen, both of them must be very careful not to bring their friendship into the workplace, which would be considered extremely unprofessional. In some cultures bosses play a parental role vis-à-vis their employees, assuming a certain amount of responsibility for the overall well-being of those who work under them, both on and off the job. This "father-figure" function is not part of the manager-subordinate relationship in the United States.

Subordinates, American Style

If the expectation of bosses is that they will be hands-off, then the expectation of subordinates is that they will be able to handle all the freedom.

Employees who are not going to be managed, in short, had better be able to manage themselves. And the qualities that make that possible — being self-reliant, creative, proactive, a problem solver, able to take responsibility, and, above all, being a "self-starter," someone who does not need a great deal of supervision and support — are the qualities that are most admired and rewarded in the American workplace.

By contrast, the worst thing a worker can be in the United States is "needy" or what is sometimes known as an HME, a high maintenance employee. HMEs, as the name suggests, are those individuals who more or less turn the ideal manager-subordinate relationship on its head, needing very close supervision and a great deal of support. "HMEs are so concerned about making mistakes or being blamed for something," Stephen Viscusi writes in *On the Job,*

> that they're incapable of showing initiative, applying creativity, or working things out with other employees on their own. The manager is constantly drawn in to every deliberation, asked for guidance on every step, no matter how trivial. Delegating to an HME increases a manager's workload, rather than decreases it. (2001, 42, 43)

As Viscusi suggests, bosses expect employees to get along with each other. Subordinates are supposed to be professionals, and that means they should be able to set aside personal feelings and differences of opinion and work together to get the job done. Of all the tasks hands-off bosses want to keep their hands off of, surely dealing with interpersonal conflicts is at the top of the list.

Taking Initiative

Subordinates who are given responsibility are expected to exercise it, to think for themselves, make decisions, take risks, and not be afraid to make or admit to mistakes. In their book *If it ain't broken, break it,* Robert Kriegel and Louis Patler tell the story of Jim Burke, a director at the American pharmaceutical company Johnson and Johnson, one of whose

> first stabs at innovation, upon becoming head of the new products division, was a children's chest rub. It failed miserably, and Burke worried that

he might not get a second chance. "Are you the one who just cost us all that money?" asked J&J chairman General Robert Wood Johnson. "Well, I just want to congratulate you. If you are making mistakes, that means you are making decisions and taking risks, and we won't grow unless you take risks." (1991, 197)

Speaking Up

Subordinates are expected to form their own opinions (not simply repeat those of the boss) and express themselves freely. If the practice of delegating is going to work, then bosses need honest assessments of those matters that have been delegated and about which subordinates, after all, know much more than their superiors. This is especially true in those cases where the subordinate's view or assessment of a situation or a practice may differ from that of the boss. If a subordinate disagrees with the boss, thinks the boss is wrong, or hasn't understood something, he or she is expected to say so, albeit tactfully and at the right moment. Bosses are always free to disregard what subordinates say in such situations — supervisors always have the final say — but subordinates are expected to express any reservations, concerns, or differing opinions. In the end, bosses can only make good decisions if they have good information, but if subordinates pull their punches in their interactions with superiors, then bosses may never get the information they need. "Associates who do not concur with the decisions being made during meetings have a responsibility to speak up," Perry Smith has written. "By remaining silent during these discussions, they do the leader a grave disservice. A major part of the associates' duties is to speak out on issues, particularly when they disagree . . ." (2002, 37).

It's true, of course, that insecure or weak bosses may prefer subordinates who tell them what they want to hear and who never disagree with them, but the best bosses want the truth and tend not to take disagreements personally. These bosses usually have a nose for people who are trying to curry favor with them and tend to keep them at a safe distance. Coworkers, meanwhile, look down on colleagues who "suck up" to managers by always agreeing with them.

All of the above notwithstanding, subordinates should still be careful how they go about disagreeing with a boss or telling her she's wrong.

Bosses have feelings too, and it is no more appropriate to hurt a supervisor's feelings than it is to hurt anyone else's. A meeting or any other public venue is almost never the right place to disagree with a boss. And even when you are in the right place, remember that your goal is not so much to point out that the boss is wrong as it is to provide the right information (and let the boss figure out the rest).

How Americans See Others

In many cultures *power* is not such a dirty word. In his famous study of IBM mentioned earlier, the Dutch sociologist Geert Hofstede distinguished between what he called low- and high-"power distance" cultures, depending on how comfortable people in a given culture were with the unequal distribution of power and influence that is common to all societies. In high-power-distance cultures, people accept inequality in power and influence quite readily; bosses closely guard their power and rarely delegate (although authority is often delegated on paper), and subordinates expect and want to be micromanaged. As you might imagine, the United States ranked low on power distance in Hofstede's survey: number 38 out of 50 countries or in the bottom fourth (1991, 26).

Empowered American subordinates do not take kindly to high-power-distance bosses who closely guard their authority. They come across as power hungry, aloof, and dominating, and accordingly they inspire little or no respect (although, ironically, they seem to crave it). They can also come across as insecure and easily threatened; they don't share information, for example, or encourage open communication up and down the ranks. Such bosses get upset when an American disagrees with them, and they don't like it when someone goes to a subordinate for a decision, tries to use his or her own judgment or initiative, or doesn't keep the boss informed of the most minor matters.

Since these high-power-distance bosses tend to micromanage and not delegate, Americans conclude that either they don't trust their subordinates or they don't think much of their abilities. Either way, their meddling and second-guessing undermine morale and motivation and stifle creativity. If these managers also seem to expect special treatment, to be deferred to, for example, or be called by their title, or if they act as if they're above doing certain things, then they run the additional risk of coming across as arrogant and egotistical.

Meanwhile, Americans tend to see the subordinates in these cultures as browbeaten, timid, and lacking in self-confidence. They say whatever their bosses want to hear, are obsessed with being polite and respectful, and refuse to take any responsibility. Americans who manage such subordinates are frustrated and annoyed by their apparent lack of initiative, by their need for constant supervision and guidance, by their apparent paranoia about making mistakes, and by their unwillingness to take even the most routine actions without first checking with the boss.

Americans think subordinates from high-power-distance cultures can't be entirely trusted. They don't ask questions when they should, don't speak up when they haven't understood or don't agree with something, and don't ask for help when they need it. When they are confronted with a mistake, they have the temerity to blame the manager for not giving better instructions or closer supervision. Their behavior is altogether too passive and sycophantic for the typical American boss.

American bosses get frustrated when high-power-distance types come to them for decisions about matters that are decided further down the chain of command, usually by middle managers. The people who approach these bosses believe they are being polite and respectful, of course, but to the Americans, who really do delegate down, it's a waste of time to have to hear these people out and then send them to the real decision makers.

Americans are also very frustrated by bosses from more particularist cultures where people take very good care of their ingroup. These bosses tend to give ingroup members preferential treatment and to reward loyalty much more highly than performance. Americans find these bosses unfair and feel undervalued when their achievements don't seem to count for anything.

Quick Tips:
Advice for Working with Americans

Managers

- Don't "act superior":
  - don't insist on deference or formality from your employees.
  - be accessible, available to talk with subordinates whenever they need to see you.
  - never act as if you're "above" (too important to do) certain menial tasks.
- Don't be upset if employees disagree with you or give you their "input"; they're not being disrespectful.
- Don't be afraid to delegate authority and responsibility; hoarding your power is taken as a sign of weakness and a lack of confidence in subordinates.
- Do *not* micromanage your employees:
  - don't second-guess decisions you have empowered them to make.
  - don't expect them to check with you before taking routine actions.
  - don't insist on being kept informed about all the details of what they are doing.
  - let subordinates try things even if they might fail.
  - encourage open discussion and feedback.
  - don't become defensive if someone disagrees with you.

Subordinates

- Expect general but not specific guidance from your boss; you will usually be told what to do, but you will be expected to decide how to do it on your own.
- Keep your boss informed of the "big picture" but not all the details of what you do.
- If something has been delegated to you, you can usually act on that matter without getting permission from your boss.

(*continued*)

- It's okay, one-on-one, to question your boss or express disagreement.
- Bosses don't expect you to agree with everything they say; they want — and need — your honest feedback (but not in a way that embarrasses them or undermines their authority).
- Don't be too worried about making mistakes; most bosses prefer employees who use initiative and exercise their own judgment.

PART 2

The Details

What strikes me the most upon the whole is the total difference of manners between them and us, from the greatest object to the least. There is not the smallest similitude in the twenty-four hours. It is obvious in every trifle.

— Horace Walpole, *Letters*

T his is the office etiquette section of this book, a list of the basic do's and don'ts of the American workplace. We're not especially concerned here with American values or beliefs or where they come from, but with what Americans actually do in a number of the most common workplace situations — and, therefore, what they'll expect *you* to do in those same situations.

Entire books and chapters of books have been written about many of the topics addressed in this section, such as meetings and presentations, to cite only two. But the goal here is to give just a brief overview of each topic, covering the basic or most common features. We won't distinguish between kinds of meetings or types of presentations, for example, but we will describe elements common to most meetings and most presentations.

Needless to say, not everyone feels the same about how to use e-mail or the telephone, for example, so the standard advice to beware of generalizations must be repeated here. Just remember that you will never meet a general person, nor will you ever be in a general situation; so use the advice given in this chapter carefully.

Workplace Relationships

Americans like to "get to know" the people they work with, by which they mean establishing something more than a purely professional relationship. They like to think of the people they work with as friends, in other words, and not just colleagues or business associates. This means they tend to be more open and familiar with coworkers, sharing personal feelings and talking freely about their private or family life. Indeed, many Americans will openly discuss matters with coworkers that people in other cultures only discuss with family members and their closest friends. Americans would find it odd if they didn't know anything about a coworker's private life after a relatively short acquaintance. This does not mean, incidentally, that it's acceptable to be talking about personal or private matters when you're supposed to be working, but American coworkers will expect you to share information about your personal life with them at other times.

Among other things, this notion that you should be "friendly" with the people at work explains the importance of small talk in the American workplace. When two Americans meet or when they talk with each other on the phone, they usually begin with a brief exchange of personal information. One might ask the other what he or she did over the weekend, ask how a spouse or child is doing, comment on the weather, or talk briefly about a common interest such as a sports team or a new movie. There is a deliberate effort, in other words, to begin conversations with something other than business, something other than the work-related topic that is the purpose of the phone call or appointment. Needless to say, people who immediately begin their conversations with business are usually seen by Americans as unfriendly.

The content of small talk should not be anything too serious or too complicated or anything that takes very much time; that's what makes it "small." In fact, the speakers are not really talking *about* anything, not listening that closely to each other; it's just a ritual exchange, the real content of which is the message that since we're friends, we can't start talking about business immediately.

American small talk should not be confused with the custom in many Latin American, African, and Middle Eastern societies of avoiding business altogether in the first meeting with a prospective client or supplier and focusing instead on establishing trust and personal rapport. American small talk is very brief, just a minute or two, and is always followed by getting down to business.

Perhaps because they are such a mobile people, Americans are also more likely to *become* friends with their coworkers than are people from many other parts of the world. In much of Europe, for example, one's friends are more likely to be lifelong acquaintances met at an early age, and it is relatively rare to socialize with people from work or to work with people from one's social circle. In contrast, the people Americans spend their time with after work and on weekends are very often some of the same people they see every day on the job; many Americans even date and eventually marry people they meet at work.

This blurring of the distinction between coworkers and friends in the United States makes the American workplace seem much more social than that in many other countries, and likewise means that the world of work often looms much larger in personal relationships and social settings. People often talk about personal problems on the job, although they're not supposed to do so "on company time" (see Personal and Professional below), and about work-related problems or personalities when they are away from the job.

Because the workplace dynamic is inevitably more personalized in the United States, cliques or associations of friends tend to form. People look out for each other, take sides, defend their friends, and sometimes even let personal feelings interfere with their professional judgments, although most people try very hard not to do this.

It is ironic that in a society where people work with friends and socialize with coworkers, it is considered the height of unprofessionalism to let personal feelings interfere in any way with one's conduct on the job. It is okay to have friends among one's coworkers, but it is not okay to treat those friends differently from anyone else. Americans are quite sensitive about this and very alert to the slightest sign that a personal relationship may be influencing a person's judgments or decisions. Indeed, they often go out of their way to avoid even the appearance of impartiality in their professional interactions. "If the friend beset by domestic trouble is a member of a project team you're heading up," Stephen Viscusi writes,

> and has been unable to carry his share of the load, and therefore is jeopardizing the project, you have no choice but to replace him. If he's a professional, he'll understand and not hold it against you. . . . When business and friendship conflict on the job, business trumps friendship every time. (2001, 119, 120)

This is especially true in the case of manager-subordinate friendships, which, for this very reason, are relatively rare in the workplace.

Personal and Professional

Apart from obvious exceptions such as emergencies, you should never let personal and/or family matters interfere with or otherwise affect your performance at work. A personal or family problem, in other words, is almost never an acceptable explanation or excuse for something you have done or not done at the office, such as missing an important meeting or not finishing a report on time.

Americans are not unfeeling, of course; if you miss a meeting because your daughter's daycare arrangement fell through or because the neighbor who drives your mother to her weekly dialysis is feeling under the weather — if things happen that are clearly beyond your control, everyone will understand. At the same time, however, you will be expected to sort out these issues so that they don't continue to spill over into your work life — finding a backup driver for your mother, for example, or making more reliable arrangements for daycare.

In the same way, it's generally not acceptable to spend work time conducting personal or family business, such as making plans for a weekend trip, consoling your distraught brother on the breakup of his latest romance, or scheduling a babysitter for Friday night. You can do these things over lunch if you like — lunch time is usually considered personal time — or on a break, but not when you should be working. At the same time, employers know that some personal business, such as talking on the phone to your mother's doctor or to your child's teacher, can't always be scheduled around work. As much as possible, however, you will be expected to deal with personal matters "on your *own* time," as Americans say, not on company time. Whenever dealing with personal or family issues takes you away from your workplace, the time you are gone will probably be charged against your vacation or sick leave (or you will be expected to make that time up by coming in early or working late).

The other side of the personal/professional separation is that when work is over, it's over. Employers who expect workers not to use company time for personal matters can't very well expect you to give up personal

time for company matters. If your boss wants you to stay late to participate in a conference call or meet with a client, you may choose to do so
as a favor (or as a good career move), but you are under no obligation to
do so.

Women in the Workplace

Women hold positions at every level in the workplace, from entry-level support staff to division heads to CEOs. They occupy close to 45 percent of the country's management positions, although they make up less than 5 percent of senior executives (Kim 2001, 50).

In general, there are no special instructions for how women should be treated in the workplace; they should be treated the same as men. Most women would strenuously object to being treated "special" simply because they are female, and would be insulted (at best) to be held to different standards from men. In general, then, the proper way to treat a woman in a particular position in the workplace is the way you would treat a man in that same position. It's especially important, for example, not to automatically expect a woman in the workplace to perform certain tasks that are more closely associated with women outside the workplace, such as arranging the catering for an office event, preparing coffee in the morning, or cleaning up the office kitchen. If these tasks would not be expected of a man holding a particular job, they should not be expected of a woman in that same job.

In the same way, assumptions should not be made about what women should not or cannot do in the workplace based on those tasks women are typically not expected to perform in society at large. Women should not be automatically shielded or somehow protected from "men's work," in other words, they should be consulted. Some women, of course, will be quite happy to serve coffee and not have to ask strangers to leave the property; the advice here is to always consult the individual involved (whether man or woman) and not make assumptions based solely on gender.

There is a tradition in some regions of the world, especially in Latin America and the Middle East, to treat women with what might be called elaborate courtesy, such as standing when they enter the room, pulling out their chair when they sit down, opening doors for them, or otherwise treating women as the "weaker" sex. While some American women may appreciate these courtesies and not be offended, others may find such behavior condescending or patronizing. Men from these regions of the world should not assume that all women will react favorably to these practices.

Sexual harassment (see next section) is an extremely serious issue in the American workplace, and the evidence is clear that many Americans — to say nothing of non-Americans — don't fully understand what constitutes harassment. Cultural differences only complicate the matter, of course, and you as a non-American are strongly advised to educate yourself thoroughly on the subject.

Sexual Harassment

The issue of sexual harassment is something of a cultural minefield for non-Americans working in the American workplace. In many cases, behavior that would be appropriate and acceptable or, at the very least, not offensive in your home culture might constitute harassment in the United States. The best rule of thumb here is to be sure you are well informed and very clear about what constitutes harassment on the job in America.

In the broadest sense, harassment is defined as any behavior that creates what is known as a "hostile work environment." Actions that fall into this category, according to the legislation, are any offensive behavior[s] that would make an employee uncomfortable and that interfere with their work performance. This definition includes a wide variety of behaviors:

1. Any demand for sexual favors from a superior to a subordinate
2. Any suggestive remarks that strongly imply or state an interest in a sexual encounter or relationship
3. Obscene or lewd comments, jokes, conversations, or non-verbal communication that embarrass, upset, or offend the listener
4. Any inappropriate, unwanted physical contact or touching, other than a handshake
5. Lewd or obscene images displayed in a prominent place or the playing of lewd music within earshot of someone who doesn't want to hear it
6. Compliments that seem to have a sexual overtone

Sexual harassment counselors even advise people who are close friends, who typically embrace, hug, or touch each other when they meet socially, to limit physical contact to a handshake in the workplace.

The definition of harassment notwithstanding, it is a very subjective and personal phenomenon; what would be considered harassment to one person might be acceptable to another. Moreover, it is often the way something is said or done rather than the actual words or behavior that constitutes harassment. If you have any doubt about whether a particular behavior might constitute harassment, be sure to make inquiries before acting. Sexual harassment is a serious matter.

Meetings

Americans are highly conflicted about meetings; they schedule and attend lots of them — meetings take up more than half the work week for many professionals — and they complain about almost all of them. From a cultural perspective, this ambivalence isn't that hard to understand; meetings appeal to one key American value, the efficient use of time, and conflict with two others, individualism (meetings are group events) and a strong preference for doing over talking (meetings are almost all talk). For an American, then, the best meetings are those that are not a minute longer than they have to be; almost everything that is good about a good meeting stems from this simple premise.

The first rule of meetings, the so-called "send a memo" rule, is not to call them if you don't need them. As you plan your meeting, ask yourself if people need to be together in the same room to accomplish what you have in mind. This is especially true of what are known as information meetings, where the main purpose is to inform people of recent developments or decisions, a new procedure or policy, or otherwise make some kind of announcement. If the objective of your meeting could be accomplished just as well in a memo or an e-mail, then it should be. Many meetings are multipurpose, of course, with an information component followed by the give-and-take discussion that does require having people together in the same room. In those instances, be sure to keep the information/announcement part as brief as possible (or better yet, do it ahead of time in a memo).

The next rule about meetings is not to schedule them too soon. Many meetings turn out to be premature; the participants arrive only to discover that before they can do whatever they have been called together to do, someone needs to make a certain decision, certain information has to be collected, or a certain person needs to be consulted on a certain topic. And none of these things has happened yet. These meetings can't really proceed, and they end up wasting a lot of people's time.

The next thing to get right about a meeting is to invite only those people who need to be there. You can only do this if you've got a very precise agenda and you circulate it to potential attendees ahead of time.

When they see the agenda, they should be able to decide whether they have to attend or if they need to contact you for clarification. If you change the agenda before the meeting, be sure to let everyone know.

It's also a good idea to put times next to each agenda item, indicating how long you think it should take or how much time you're going to allow to discuss that item. Participants may exceed the allotted time by a few minutes, but at least they will know how long they're supposed to be spending on each item and when they've gone over the limit.

The thing that probably annoys Americans the most at a meeting is when people get off the subject. If you're running the meeting, you have to catch this as soon as you see it happening and stop it immediately; if you're an attendee, be sure to stick to the point. A related danger, and probably the second most annoying thing that can happen at a meeting from the American perspective, is when someone goes on too long about something. Strictly speaking, this person has not gotten off the subject, but he or she is providing much more detail, background information, or context than the rest of the group needs to understand and/or act on the matter under discussion. This transgression of meeting etiquette is harder to detect but no less serious and should never be indulged.

Allowing people to get off the subject and to go on too long about something are the two greatest threats to most meetings and the two most common complaints heard about bad meetings. If you get nothing else about your meeting right, be sure to keep these two things from happening. As far as can be determined, no American has ever complained that a meeting ended too soon.

Keep the meeting moving. Watch the clock carefully (everyone else will be), and keep the meeting on schedule by not exceeding the time for each agenda item. If the time allotted for an item is not realistic, point this out and ask the participants what they want to do now. They can decide to stay on the issue until it is resolved, which will extend the meeting beyond its promised length; they can continue the discussion and drop subsequent items, ending the meeting on time; or they can cut off the discussion, staying on schedule, and agree to have another meeting on this topic. Giving attendees the choice in these cases is always better than simply letting the discussion continue and assuming no one minds if the meeting gets out late. *Everyone* minds, even those who are the reason it's getting out late!

In his book on leadership, General Perry Smith cites what might be called the "11 AM rule" for meetings. Any meeting scheduled for one hour that starts at 11 AM almost always finishes on time because most attendees already have lunch plans (2002, 259).

In some cultures meetings are more of a ritual, in the sense that most of what is "discussed" and decided upon has already been agreed to earlier in a series of one-on-one conversations. The meeting is then something of a formality where details may be talked about but where there is very little serious discussion of anything substantial. This approach is common in more collective, group-oriented cultures where group harmony and saving face are key values, and it is therefore important that disagreements and differences of opinion never become public.

You should know that this is generally not the case in American meetings. While the issues to be discussed have no doubt been talked about before the meeting, one of the primary purposes of most meetings is precisely to give all participants a chance to express their opinions, discuss their differences, and come to an agreement. There is, in short, a great deal of what Americans call "give and take" at a meeting; participants are expected to openly express their disagreements and to honestly say what they think of each other's opinions and suggestions. They are expected to be polite and not hurt another person's feelings, but they are also expected to say what they think. It is true, of course, that even Americans sometimes "pull their punches" at meetings, saying what they think other people, especially the higher ups, want to hear.

A final word of warning: the customary cross-cultural advice — observe closely what the local people do and then try to imitate them — does *not* apply in the case of meetings; many Americans aren't very good at running them. Leadership guru Perry Smith has described the American "cultural tendency to hold long, undisciplined meetings that yield little useful output" (*Rules and Tools for Leaders,* 2002, 11). This lack of discipline no doubt stems in part from that low-profile, hands-off management style described earlier, which makes it difficult for Americans to take on the role of the enforcer, a role essential for a good chairperson.

Presentations

Presentations have been alluded to several times in these pages, usually in the context of how important it is to keep them simple and quickly get to the point. These are, in fact, probably the two most important things to keep in mind when designing and delivering a presentation to Americans. Another closely related point is never to forget that when people come to your presentation, they have chosen to turn over some of their extremely limited time to you, so you had better not waste it.

In designing a presentation, remember that less is always more as far as Americans are concerned, meaning you should always err on the side of saying too little rather than too much. The point is not to say everything you know about your topic but only what the audience needs to hear, and an American audience usually only wants to hear enough to be able to make an informed decision about the matter at hand. Generally they don't expect a lot of background information — about methodology, or about the history of the project, study, or proposal — or a lot of details. In a presentation, Americans typically want what they call "the big picture"; they can always get back to you for more information if they need it (or this information can be provided in handouts for people to read later).

In some cases, of course, understanding the background information is essential to understanding your main points. In those instances, it's always a good idea to state those main points at the beginning of your talk and then present the background information. Unless they see "where you're going" with your talk, Americans get impatient; if you start with where you're going, they'll relax and pay closer attention.

Keep it practical. By and large the main thing Americans want to hear from you is So what? How does this affect me? What am I supposed to do with or do about what you're telling me? Why am I in this room today listening to you? Americans aren't necessarily interested in knowledge or information for its own sake but more for how they can apply it. Whatever the content of your presentation, whatever points you're going to make in your talk, be sure to explain how the people in the room can use this information when they go back to their desks. In other words, make it personal.

On a closely related matter, keep it concrete. Americans don't relate well to abstractions, theories, concepts, or paradigms. They understand them and their importance, but they respond better to illustrations, examples, statistics — anything that grounds the abstract in the real and the practical.

Remember: your presentation is about the audience, not about you and your content. Watch your audience very closely; if you see that people are "getting it," that they have understood your point, then immediately move on to your next point. The idea is not to say everything you had planned to say, but to say no more than you need to.

Start and end with a bang. The weakest parts of most presentations are those that need to be the strongest: the opening and the closing. For obvious reasons, most presenters carefully prepare the body of their presentation, their main points, and only prepare their opening and closing if they have time. But a strong opening and closing can make all the difference.

You need to get people's attention right away, and the quickest way to do that is to say something very interesting almost immediately. Many speakers begin with the objectives of their presentation, and while these may be marginally important, they certainly aren't interesting. Or they begin with an overview of what they're going to talk about, following the classic (bad) advice of "Begin by telling the audience what you're going to tell them." People don't want to know what you're *going* to say; they want you to start saying it. You should begin with an fascinating story or anecdote, a dramatic statistic, or "the best piece of advice" you were ever given. You can't talk to people until you've gotten their attention.

The same goes for the ending, which should be planned to make the maximum impact; it is, after all, the last thing people will hear before they walk out of the room. So make it memorable. Ideally, it would be a well-phrased, succinct restatement of your main point, preceded or followed, perhaps, by another interesting story or statistic.

Humor works, but be careful. Most American listeners like to be entertained, and most find humor entertaining, but a presenter has to use humor carefully. Many presenters begin with a joke, but this isn't always a good idea. For one thing, many in the audience will be reluctant to laugh at the joke, even if they think it's funny, for fear they might be the only one who thinks so. For another, many jokes make fun of a certain kind of person or a certain group, and there may be people of that type or group in the audience. Finally, much humor is very culture-specific; before you tell a joke or funny story to an American audience, try it out on an American acquaintance to see if it is really funny. The only kind of humor that seems to be almost foolproof is a funny story about yourself.

Many presentations prompt questions or include a question-and-answer session at the end. Presenters should be very careful how they handle questions, whether they take them during the presentation itself or at the end. The rule to remember is that in most cases the vast majority of the audience is not interested in any particular question. To put it another way, as soon as you begin answering someone's question, you have lost the attention of most of the other people in the room. So if you're going to take questions during your presentation, limit your answer to 30 seconds or less.

Even if you limit questions to a Q-and-A session at the end of your talk, which is highly recommended, you still have to be careful. Remember that the main thing time-deprived, time-challenged Americans want to do at the end of your presentation is to get out of the room. So if you're holding a Q-and-A session, invite those who want to leave to do so before you start. And even then, keep your answers short.

Want to be a hero? In closing I offer the one piece of absolutely foolproof advice about giving a presentation to Americans: end it early.

E-mail Etiquette

E-mail has revolutionized the workplace; the average worker in the United States now spends almost one-fourth of his or her day (one hour and 45 minutes) writing or reading e-mail. It has become such a central part of life on the job that it is important for non-Americans to understand the basic conventions of e-mail use in the American workplace.

The place to begin is by noting that most people are overwhelmed by e-mail; it's just too easy to communicate that way (also too quick and too cheap). If e-mail were simply a substitute for making telephone calls — if people sent only the messages they used to call about — it wouldn't be a problem. The average worker would still receive more or less the same amount of information in a typical day, but it would come in a different form. But e-mail is not used like that; people send all manner of messages by e-mail that they would never send if they had to convey the same information in a telephone call. In short, e-mail means people no longer have to be selective about the messages they send — and most people are not.

The first rule of e-mail use, then, is that less is definitely more. Before writing a message, apply the telephone test referred to above by asking yourself, If I had to call someone with this information or question, would I? If the answer is no, then at the very least that message is probably not urgent, although it may still be important, and you may want to label it accordingly (which most e-mail programs now allow you to do).

Which brings us to the second rule of e-mail etiquette: always complete the subject box. While people can't control the number of messages they receive, they *can* control the number of messages they open, but only if the subject box is filled in. And even then, it has to be filled in carefully. Simply writing From Bill, Heads Up, or For Your Information (FYI) doesn't tell recipients what they most need to know, which is Do I need to read this e-mail? and/or Can this e-mail wait? Even e-mail users who are good at filling in the subject box often forget to do so when they reply to someone else's e-mail, leaving the sender's subject intact, which is usually not helpful to the recipient.

Be very selective about who you copy on your messages. If sending an e-mail is easy, copying others is simplicity itself. People already receive too many messages they *have* to read, so don't bombard them with messages they don't have to read (but may feel guilty if they do not).

Be equally selective about attachments: Always make brief mention of any attachments in the text of the e-mail so recipients know whether or not they need to open them (or which ones they may need to open). If the attachments are all FYI, or if some are FYI and some are not, be sure to indicate this.

Composing E-mails

Assuming that people are going to send e-mails they should not and recipients are going to open ones they need not, the least senders can do is to keep their messages brief and easy to read. Come to the point quickly and don't go on any longer than necessary. To make your messages easier to read and to scan, limit each paragraph to one or two sentences and leave two spaces between them. Use ALL CAPITALS very sparingly, as words written in that form are hard to read and are considered the e-mail equivalent of shouting.

In the United States, an e-mail is considered a relatively informal means of communication, certainly as compared to a letter. E-mail writers usually don't worry much about good grammar and punctuation, about writing complete sentences, or in some cases even checking their spelling.

And the tone of American e-mails is likewise very informal. Americans seem to feel that it's okay to "think out loud" in an e-mail, trying out a particular line of reasoning, groping toward a decision, or otherwise fumbling with words and feelings in full view of the recipient. What one says in an e-mail, in short, does not always have to be fully thought out or the sender's last word on the particular subject. There is also the sense that one is not as accountable for what one writes in an e-mail as for what one says face-to-face or in a letter. Not surprisingly, then, already direct Americans tend to edit themselves even less in e-mails than face-to-face, offering up surprisingly blunt and candid opinions and almost instant reactions.

Answering E-mails

Because they receive so many e-mails, most people are not able to respond to all their messages on the day they receive them, unlike voice-mails, for example, which one should always try to return the same day. Because this is widely understood, only urgent e-mails need to be answered immediately, and most e-mail programs label these messages accordingly. For the rest, it is acceptable to answer an e-mail anywhere from one to two days after it is received. If you think it's going to take you longer to answer a message, then it's considered good form to respond briefly in a short note acknowledging receipt and promising to get back to the sender as soon as possible.

Many messages don't require an answer, of course, and many others are in a discretionary category; while they don't require an answer, the sender would probably appreciate knowing you got the information or the attachment. If you have time, it's a good idea to acknowledge these messages with a quick thank you. Remember that e-mail messages may be the only impressions many people ever have of you, and like all impressions, you want to them to be positive. If you come across as polite and considerate via e-mail, you are doing yourself a favor.

Telephone Etiquette

As noted in the e-mail section, Americans have come to regard the telephone quite differently since the advent of the Internet. Whereas it was formerly used for anything that couldn't be done by regular mail, its use has become much more selective now that e-mail is such a convenient communication option. In general, the rule seems to be to use the telephone only in cases where (1) the matter is too complex to be quickly presented in an e-mail; (2) there needs to be a genuine, real-time discussion of the matter, involving give and take by both parties; (3) the matter is too confidential or sensitive to be written about in an e-mail; or (4) the matter is too urgent to wait for an e-mail reply. Broadly speaking, these are the kinds of issues for which Americans use, and expect others to use, the telephone.

Because it has become less common, a telephone call has become more significant; if someone has called, it must be important — and if the matter is not especially important, then that someone should not have called. The one exception to this, when people call "just to talk," proves the rule; because they no longer regularly speak to each other as a natural part of doing business or working together, Americans sometimes feel the need to call merely, as they put it, "to hear the other person's voice."

So the first rule of telephone etiquette is to use the telephone carefully and sparingly. The second is to use it efficiently, respecting those two core American communication norms of getting to the point of your call quickly after the mandatory small talk (see Workplace Relationships on page 146) and of staying on the subject. Whether face-to-face or on the phone, Americans don't like conversations that go on any longer than necessary. Phone calls are trickier in this regard, because while you can always signal your impatience (or pick up on the other person's) via nonverbal behavior in a face-to-face exchange, this is much harder to do over the phone. In fact, interrupting the other speaker is practically the only way, and for this reason it is typically more tolerated in telephone conversations.

It's important to remember that a phone call is by definition an interruption, in other words, something that was not on the other person's schedule, and it is only good manners to acknowledge this. This is why Americans often begin phone conversations by asking, "Is this a good time?" or "Have you got a minute?" and why it is even acceptable (though not common) to answer, "No it isn't" and reschedule the call if necessary. The fact that it is an interruption is another reason it is even more important to get to the point and stay focused in a phone call. Whenever possible, many people now actually schedule their phone calls, usually via e-mail, so that they are no longer an interruption.

Voice Mail

People aren't always in, of course, and you then have the option of leaving a message on their voice mail. Once again the etiquette here involves being efficient; the best voice-mail messages are those that don't have to be returned. Never just leave your name and number; this is impolite and is the last kind of voice-mail message that will be answered. If you're calling in response to an earlier conversation (or voice-mail message), always try to leave a message that resolves the issue or answers the question so that the other party doesn't have to call you back.

For this same reason, when you're initiating the contact, always explain in your message why you have called so that the other person can, where possible, resolve the matter in an e-mail or in the return phone call *even if you're not in,* and so they can also decide how quickly they need to call you back. Busy people often have several voice mails waiting for them when they get to their office, and it helps them if they can prioritize their return calls. Similarly, if there's something the other person needs to do or find out before the two of you next talk, so that your business can be resolved at that time, be sure to mention that in your message. Otherwise, the return call simply sets up the necessity for yet another call.

Always give your phone number. When you leave a voice-mail message, never assume the other person knows your phone number (except in cases where it would be silly not to) or that she or he can easily look it up. People can access their voice mail from almost anywhere in the world, and they may not have your telephone number with them. If you want people to call you back, make it possible for them to do so. And be sure, incidentally, to speak slowly and clearly when you say your number.

Returning Calls

You should return voice-mail messages promptly. This is especially true in the e-mail era, when phone calls are generally assumed to be more urgent than they once were. If you don't have time to talk to the caller at length, you should at least acknowledge receiving the voice mail, either in an e-mail or in a quick return call in which you explain that you don't have time to talk "right now" but you got the message and you'll be back in touch as soon as possible.

If you call someone about a matter that is not particularly urgent and leave a voice message, be sure to indicate the low priority of your call so the recipient knows how quickly he or she has to call back.

As in most societies, there is a pecking order when it comes to returning phone calls. People are expected to return calls from higher-ups more promptly than calls from people below them in the chain of command.

Taking Calls

Taking a phone call while you're meeting with someone else is generally considered rude, and you should either ask permission to take the call or take it and apologize for doing so. In either case, try to end it as soon as possible. Senior people can take a call in the presence of subordinates, but generally colleagues should not do it with each other unless the call is urgent, the caller is a very important person (VIP), or you're just chatting with someone. If you are the "other" person in this situation, it is always polite to ask whether you should step out of the office until the phone call is over.

Telephone Tips for Speakers of English as a Second Language

If you speak English as a second language and are not fluent, you may find talking on the phone to an American difficult. In face-to-face exchanges, you can read the other person's body language and get a good idea of what that person is saying even if you don't understand all the words. This is not possible over the telephone, of course, so nonnative speakers of English may want to try a few techniques to make telephone conversations more successful. The first is to ask the other person to slow down and/or repeat what he or she has said. Americans typically don't make adjustments in their speech for nonnative speakers, but they will almost always slow down if you ask them to. Another technique is for you to repeat what the American has said and then ask if you have understood correctly. If you think you may not have understood correctly or you want to verify what was said in a phone call, you can always send the person an e-mail after your conversation, summarizing your understanding of the exchange.

If you speak English with an accent, some Americans will have trouble understanding you. You may want to slow down in such cases; another good idea is to acknowledge that you speak with an accent and invite the American to ask you to repeat anything he or she did not understand. This will be much appreciated as monolingual Americans often feel embarrassed to suggest to a non-American, who has after all learned the American's language, that he or she is difficult to understand.

Also keep this advice in mind when leaving voice mails for Americans: slow down your speech and try to speak as clearly as possible, perhaps even repeating key pieces of information twice.

Giving Feedback

People spend a lot of time on the job telling other people what they think of their work, in general (as in a performance evaluation) and in particular (as in commenting on a specific report or presentation).

As might be expected, Americans are relatively direct in giving negative feedback, although not as direct as Germans, for example, or Israelis. Even so, they almost always preface negative feedback by saying something positive.

The next rule in giving negative feedback is to be specific, to identify as precisely as possible what the other person has done that is not satisfactory, and to follow that with a clear explanation of what he or she needs to do to meet your expectations. That person needs to be in a position to respond to the feedback, in other words, and should always be given an opportunity to do so. It is unacceptable in the American workplace to give negative feedback without giving people a chance to correct what they have done wrong.

Nor is it appropriate to give negative feedback through a third person, as in some cultures, to avoid confrontation, embarrassment, or loss of face. An American will be quite upset to hear from another person that you are not pleased with his or her work, especially if you are that person's manager.

Positive feedback is very common in the American workplace, so common that people from some cultures feel that Americans overdo it. Be that as it may, Americans are used to it, expect it, and will interpret the absence of routine positive feedback (especially from a boss) as a sign that they're not doing a very good job or that their supervisor is not happy with them.

The key word here is "routine." By and large, positive feedback in the American workplace is not reserved just for those occasions when people have exceeded all expectations or otherwise done an outstanding job; it is used on a much more regular basis when people have simply done more or less what was expected of them. The feedback at such times is not lavish or effusive, but it is not unusual. Americans wouldn't be surprised, for example, to be praised for getting a report in on time or for how well they ran a meeting or handled a certain situation, even when doing those things well is simply part of their job.

Needless to say, when a worker's performance is truly out of the ordinary he or she expects even more positive feedback.

Training

Americans spend a lot of time in training or, as they sometimes call it, employee development. You may either be trained to do certain aspects of your current job better or, when you change jobs or are promoted, to learn how to do your new job. On occasion, people are sent to training to have their attitude adjusted.

There are many kinds of training, but there are a handful of norms that trainees are expected to observe in most training sessions. The first is to actively participate. American-style training is usually highly interactive, with a minimum of lecture and a maximum of trainee involvement, whether it's small-group discussion, problem-solving activities, role playing, simulations, or any number of other training techniques. In this context it is often said that trainees should "take responsibility for their own learning," by which is meant get involved, ask questions, participate. It is for this reason, incidentally, that trainers in the United States are often called "facilitators," meaning they aren't necessarily content experts, the people with all the answers; they are, rather, "expert" at getting the answers out of the trainees.

Clearly then, you are not expected to be a passive observer; it is okay to challenge trainers, to question them, and to get into lively discussions with them (although not to monopolize the discussion). You are also expected to be open and somewhat flexible, to be receptive to new ideas and other opinions, and to suspend judgment on occasion, such as on something the trainer may ask you to do when you do not understand the reason.

Trainees are not expected to pull their punches during training; they should state their views openly and give their honest opinions (without, of course, hurting another person's feelings). The point of many training sessions is to work on, resolve, or at least bring out into the open certain office problems or dynamics, and progress will not be made if people aren't honest with each other.

You should also be very honest in your evaluation of training. Employers spend a lot of money on a typical training event, and they want to know if the time and the funds were well spent.

Nonverbal Communication

Nonverbal communication is a discipline unto itself, and entire books have been written on the subject. Ray Birdwhistell, a pioneer in the field, estimated that the human face is capable of making more than 250,000 separate expressions (1970, 8), and researchers worldwide have identified more than 1,000 different body "attitudes" or postures that can be "maintained steadily," meaning they could be used to send a message (Luce and Smith 1987, 120). The vocabulary of the human body, in short, is much more extensive than that of the mind, and it should not be surprising that so much communication is carried on without benefit of words.

Different cultures rely to different degrees on nonverbal communication. Generally, more direct cultures such as the United States rely more on words (verbal communication), but even Americans make good use of the various types of nonverbal expression. According to Albert Mehrabian, in the United States 7 percent of the meaning of a spoken message comes from the actual meaning of the words, 38 percent from the way one says the words, and 55 percent, or more than half, from nonverbal channels such as gestures, facial expressions, and body language (Luce and Smith, 137). Another study found that 65 percent of the "social meaning of a typical two-person exchange" came from nonverbal cues (119). If more than half the messages Americans send are nonverbal, it behooves non-Americans to educate themselves on American body language.

At the same time it should be noted that compared to cultures that are even more nonverbal, such as some of the indirect cultures of the Asia-Pacific region, Americans are still *relatively* much more verbal. This means that on the whole Americans are less adept at looking for and correctly reading nonverbal communication because they are not as accustomed to expressing themselves this way. People from Japan, for example, or Thailand, who are used to saying one thing and then sending the real message through facial expressions or body posture, should not assume that Americans are even seeing these nonverbal messages, much less interpreting them correctly. Moreover, if, like the Japanese, you tend on occasion to express yourself by means of what you do *not* say, then be warned that Americans almost never hear what is not said. In the end, if you come from a culture where words are not the primary carrier of meaning and you want Americans to understand you, then you will have to learn to put more of your message in the spoken word and less in the unspoken.

Personal Space

In public Americans tend to stand somewhere between eighteen and twenty-four inches away from each other. It is said that if you make a fist and hold out your arm, it should reach to the other person's shoulder blade. Anything less, and an American will step back; anything more, and an American will step forward. It's easy to observe this norm in practice if you watch two Americans getting on an empty elevator; they will always move to the sides in order to get their eighteen inches. The eighteen-inch rule also seems to explain why Americans don't usually talk on a crowded elevator: they are standing too close to face each other, and it's awkward talking without looking at the other person. If they do talk, they tend to talk straight ahead without inclining their body toward the other person.

People from cultures with a shorter personal space norm — of ten to twelve inches, let's say, as is the case in much of the Middle East or Latin America — will stand too close to Americans, thereby coming across as aggressive or rude, while Americans who stand two feet away come across to such people as distant, reserved, and unfriendly. In the same way, people from cultures with a longer norm, two-and-a-half to three feet, will stand too far from Americans (and be seen as distant and cold), and Americans will stand too close to these people (and be seen as aggressive and rude). Finding the right distance should not be difficult. Just watch what Americans do and imitate them.

Eye Contact

Americans feel it is polite, a sign of showing interest and paying attention, to look another person in the eye when he or she is talking to them. American eye contact is not continuous in such cases — Americans will look away briefly — but it is sustained, and it applies regardless of any age difference or difference in seniority or authority between the two people in the conversation. It is true, however, that the listener will look down for part of the time if he or she is ashamed or being reprimanded by the speaker.

In some cultures it is considered impolite and aggressive to sustain eye contact with an older person, with an authority figure, or with other respected individuals. If you are from such a culture, remember that Americans will interpret your lack of eye contact (if you're the listener) as being rude and not paying attention; meanwhile, you should not interpret sustained American eye contact as a sign of aggression or impoliteness.

The speaker in a two-way conversation likewise maintains sustained eye contact; many Americans believe that if the person speaking to you does not look you in the eye, then he or she must not be telling the truth.

Touching

Americans engage in a moderate amount of physical contact with other people, more than some Europeans (such as the English) and less than people from Central and South America, for example, or Africa and the Middle East. Two women are more likely to embrace each other upon meeting than are two men, who are more likely to confine their contact to shaking hands. Two women may walk arm in arm, but men usually do not. In conversation, men or women may on occasion reach out and briefly touch the other person's forearm or knee (if they are sitting close enough and if they know each other well), but generally not if the other person is of the opposite sex.

Public displays of affection between male-female couples are generally acceptable. They can stand very close, embrace, hold hands as they walk, put their arms around each other, and kiss upon greeting or taking leave of each other. A lingering kiss in public is typically less common. Many same-sex couples engage in these same behaviors, although it is probably less common.

Men and women who are not part of a couple or not close friends engage in very little physical contact, usually nothing more than a handshake. Any other touching can easily take on sexual overtones and be considered inappropriate.

Even in crowded public spaces, such as on buses or subway cars or on elevators, you should try not to stand (or sit) in such a way that you are making physical contact with other people. If you accidentally come into contact with another person, you should apologize.

Gestures

Regarding the range of gestures Americans use, thrusting the middle finger at another person — holding your hand out, palm facing you with only the middle finger raised — is probably the most offensive.

Most Americans feel it is not polite to point at another person, although it is fine to point at objects or to indicate direction. On the other hand, pointing the index finger at another person and then beckoning him or her to approach by curling the finger in and out is generally acceptable (although many people beckon by using the whole hand in this same manner).

Two gestures with a negative connotation are shaking your fist at someone, a sign that you are upset, and the thumb-down gesture (closing four fingers and pointing down with the thumb), a sign of disapproval. Two positive gestures are the thumb-up gesture and the okay sign (making a circle with the thumb and forefinger).

Americans typically gesture with their hands and arms when they talk, although not as much as people in the Mediterranean, the Middle East, or Latin America, who can come across as "loud," emotional, or even aggressive if they gesture "too much." By the same token, people who gesture "too little," keeping their arms to their sides, often strike Americans as stiff, cold, or reserved.

Body Postures and Other Nonverbal Behavior

Some body postures and other forms of nonverbal behavior make relatively strong statements and should only be used knowingly:

- Arms folded across your chest. While this is a fairly common listening posture, it can also connote challenge or even defiance, especially among men.

- Standing with your hands in your pockets. This posture communicates extreme casualness and informality. It should not be used if you're supposed to be paying close attention to another person or in the presence of someone to whom you need to show respect.

- Leaning against the wall. Like standing with your hands in your pockets, this form of body language also communicates extreme informality. You should not stand this way if you're supposed to be paying close attention to what another person is saying or if you should be treating that person respectfully.

- Sitting with your foot resting on your knee and/or leaning back in your chair. These are two more markers of casualness and informality, relaxed postures that suggest a lack of urgency. Neither would be appropriate in situations where you want to show that you are listening closely, that you take the conversation seriously, or when you are talking to someone very senior to you (whose words are always taken seriously). In all of these cases, the proper body posture is to sit with your legs uncrossed and leaning forward in your chair.

- Looking at your watch or looking out the window. These communicate either that you are bored or that you would like to be somewhere else. In either case, they're not polite.

- Sitting down without being asked. This is a challenging form of behavior (except between close friends), suggesting that you are in control of the situation and intend to talk to the other person whether he or she wants you to or not. Asking if you may sit down is somewhat more polite but still sends the message that you intend to stay for a while. When senior people do this in a subordinate's office, it is usually not a challenge but rather an indication that the boss is not in a hurry. A subordinate would rarely do this in the boss's office, however, unless the two people have a very close relationship.

Greetings and Leave-Takings

The standard American greeting is a smile and a brief "Hello" or "How are you?" to which the response should also be brief: "Hello" or "Fine, thank you" (even if you're not fine). If people have not seen each other for some time, they will shake hands or even embrace (men less commonly than women). Men typically wait for women to extend their hand; if the woman does not, there is no handshake. Americans expect a firm handshake, involving a slight squeeze of the other person's hand, and they consider anything less to be a sign of weakness or lack of self-confidence.

Americans are very casual about greeting people when they come in to work. Essentially, they greet the people they happen to meet, but that's all. There's no need, as in some cultures, to make any special effort to seek people out expressly to greet them. The greeting itself is also quite casual, usually just "Good morning" or "How's it going?" and does not normally involve shaking hands. As noted above, the only time Americans shake hands as part of a greeting is when they have not seen each other for some time. Nor does the greeting last very long; it's usually just a few words, unless the other person indicates he or she wants to talk longer. The polite presumption is that people are busy and don't have time to chat.

A note about chatting: it is often said that Americans are too task-oriented and never take time to socialize. While Americans do socialize less than people in more collectivist/group-oriented cultures, it's not true that they never have time to chat. Americans tend to compartmentalize work time and chat time, so that they don't chat during work time or work during chat time. Good times to chat or socialize, therefore, are early in the morning before people "begin their day," as Americans put it (i.e., before the start of work time), at lunch and during breaks, before a meeting starts, or when walking down the halls or riding in an elevator together.

In some cultures it's considered impolite not to personally greet everyone when entering a room or say goodbye to everyone when leaving. This is generally not the case in the United States; Americans will greet and say goodbye to only those people they have come to see or those they happen to be standing near (unless it's a small group).

At the end of the day Americans likewise don't make any special effort to say goodbye to anyone in particular. As with greetings, they will take leave of whomever they happen to run into, but there is no need to seek people out to say goodbye. One exception would be if someone is going on a trip or will be out of the office for an extended period; in such cases, the person who will be gone will make an effort to say goodbye to key people, and others will make an effort to see this person before he or she leaves.

Dress

Dress at work is generally somewhat less formal than in many countries, depending very much, however, on the position one has, the organization one works for, and to some extent which region of the country one works in. One rule seems to be that the more contact a person has with the general public, the more formally he or she should dress. If you're going to be toiling all day inside your cubicle, interacting only with other toilers like yourself, you would not normally have to dress up. But if you're having a meeting or going to lunch with someone from outside your company or organization, or if you're going to a meeting with someone senior in your organization, someone who typically dresses more formally than you, then you may want to dress up on these occasions.

Generally, people tend to dress somewhat more formally on the East coast, in the Midwest, and in the South (though not in Florida) than they do in the West and the Southwest. Dress also tends to be somewhat more casual in smaller companies than in large, multinational corporations, and more casual in some divisions, especially information technology, than in others. On the whole, people who work for the federal government tend to dress more formally than those in the private sector.

Dress is not that hard to get right: you simply observe how the Americans around you in similar positions dress and then follow their example. And for any special situations — an interview, a meeting, a presentation, a conference, a luncheon — just ask people how you should dress. As in almost any culture, it's usually worse to be underdressed than to be overdressed; while you can usually adjust your dress "down," taking off a jacket, a scarf, or tie, it's harder to adjust "up."

Gifts

Gift giving has almost no official role in the American workplace. There are virtually no occasions where workers would be expected to give a gift to other workers — whether a boss, subordinate, or colleague — as part of their professional duty. People make friends at work, of course, and often exchange gifts in that capacity, but rarely in the context of carrying out their work-related responsibilities. Giving gifts to someone in the context of a professional relationship is against the law in many cases, may be seen as currying favor, and is widely frowned upon.

The only time you might be expected to give a gift on the job would be when the office staff gets together to buy someone a gift on his or her birthday or some other special occasion such as an impending wedding, the birth of a child, or a going-away party. Even then, the gift comes from everyone, and you are always free not to participate if you choose.

Non-Americans who are used to bringing courtesy gifts when they first meet with someone should be advised that this is not expected in the United States. In the government, senior officials are obliged to report such gifts and may not be allowed to keep them for their personal use. Non-Americans should also be advised that Americans believe it is polite to open a gift in front of the giver at the time it is offered.

(See A Guest in the Home, pages 184–85 for gift suggestions for that context.)

Taboo Topics

There are some subjects that are not appropriate to discuss with Americans. As in most cultures, anything to do with sex and sexual behavior is private and personal and is not generally discussed. Religion is another personal topic that Americans rarely talk about, except in a general way.

Politics is often cited in the same breath as religion as another taboo topic, but in fact Americans frequently talk about politics. The part of politics that is taboo is the part that is personal; while it is perfectly appropriate to talk about politics in general, about the political situation, for example, about issues in the news, or about individual politicians, it is generally not appropriate in the workplace to ask people their personal opinion of a particular political figure or their opinion on a controversial topic, and it is especially inappropriate to get into an *argument* about politics. If people volunteer their personal views on political questions, that is another matter and a sign that they are willing to take the discussion to a more personal level.

An American socialite once said, "You can never be too rich or too thin" (Faul 1999, 15). Body weight is a touchy subject in diet-crazed, calorie-obsessed America. If you can't say something flattering about a person's weight — and the only flattering comment is that a person seems to have lost weight — then don't say anything at all. Since many Americans you meet will probably be overweight, or be very sensitive about their weight, the best advice is to avoid the subject altogether in talking with Americans. Be warned that if an American remarks that he or she is trying to lose weight, you must never say, "Good for you." The only acceptable response in all such cases is, "I can't imagine why."

Age is not a taboo subject in the United States, but growing old is something many Americans definitely do not enjoy and something they try to postpone for as long as possible. The only acceptable comments about age are those that point out how young someone looks or how the other person "hasn't changed at all" since you last saw him or her. Any comments that refer even obliquely to aging, such as those about gray hair, losing hair, wrinkles, or facelifts, should be avoided.

Money is another touchy subject with Americans. It is almost never appropriate to ask people how much money they make (their salary), and likewise it is not polite to ask someone how much something cost, especially expensive items such as a car or one's house. On the other hand, Americans love to tell other people how little they paid for something if they believe they got an especially low price.

Disease and death are not exactly taboo subjects, but they can be difficult for Americans to talk about. If a person is seriously ill or dying, Americans may not want to admit the fact or talk about it, depending on the circumstances.

Abortion is a very charged topic in the United States, and it's best to avoid it altogether.

As noted elsewhere, the topics that are encompassed by the political correctness phenomenon — such as race, sexual preference, disability — are sensitive, and unless you know your way around these topics and the related vocabulary, which a non-American often does not, the best advice is to avoid them.

Going to Lunch

Americans frequently have lunch with some of their coworkers. If you go with one or more people to a restaurant, it is understood that everyone will pay for his or her own lunch.

If a group of people is going to lunch together, it would normally be considered impolite not to invite everyone who is a member of that particular group. Anyone who does not want to go is free to decline, but might be hurt if he or she is not included in the invitation. When just two people go to lunch together, there is no expectation that they should have to invite anyone else from the office.

Bosses would not necessarily expect to be invited when a group from the office goes out to lunch together, although this would not be improper. As a rule, however, a boss and a subordinate don't go to lunch together; if they do, the boss risks being accused of favoritism and the subordinate of playing up to the boss.

On special occasions, the whole office may go to lunch together. In these cases, the bill is usually divided evenly by the number of attendees, regardless of the cost of any one person's meal. If some of the attendees drink wine or alcohol, however, and others do not, it is always polite to offer to adjust the costs accordingly.

Smoking

The United States has declared war on smoking. There are no-smoking sections in most commercial establishments such as restaurants and bars; a number of states have banned smoking in restaurants altogether. Smoking is not permitted in movie theaters or most other entertainment venues; it is not allowed on airplanes or in airports (except in designated, walled-off smoking rooms); and it is no longer permitted inside many office buildings, including in the lobbies, restrooms, and corridors.

If you are invited to someone's home, you should not assume your hosts will allow you to smoke in the house. If you are invited as one member of a dinner party, it is almost certainly expected that you will not smoke. You should, however, feel free to ask the host or hostess if they mind if you step outside for a cigarette. To be safe, if you don't know whether smoking is permitted in a particular setting, assume that it's not.

A Guest in the Home

Americans are much more likely to entertain people at home than in restaurants. If you are invited to someone's home for a meal, it is common to bring something for your hosts. Typically, Americans bring flowers (presented to the hostess), a bottle of wine or liquor, or chocolates. If you ask Americans if you can "bring anything," which is considered a polite response to such an invitation, they will almost always say no (as should you if you're doing the inviting), but this is a ritualized, polite answer and should not be taken to mean that you should not bring anything.

You should ask what time you are expected, and you should be careful not to arrive more than fifteen to twenty minutes later than the time given. Americans usually receive guests in their living room or in a family room or a den (for less formal visits). They will offer drinks and snacks, which you can eat as much or as little of as you like. It is not impolite to refuse snacks, unless they are very special, something the host or hostess has prepared especially for this event, but it is somewhat unusual not to accept a drink. If you do not drink alcohol, by all means say so; this will not embarrass Americans.

If your hosts ask you to come into the kitchen while they are preparing drinks or the meal, you should not hesitate. Likewise, some Americans will want to "show you around the house," meaning take you into the various rooms, with the customary exception of the sleeping quarters, and it would be considered rude to refuse such an invitation.

Typically the conversation on such occasions, especially if spouses and others are present, does not touch upon work (since it would exclude some of the guests). The best rule of thumb concerning what to talk about is to follow the lead of your hosts and/or other Americans present. It is quite appropriate, and much appreciated, if you compliment the food, the house, and its furnishings, but don't ask how much things cost.

Your host or hostess will almost always offer you a second helping of food (or may even encourage you to "help yourself"). If you are still hungry, by all means accept the offer, but if you are not, it is quite acceptable to decline. If you are unable to eat certain foods or ingredients (such as alcohol) for health or religious reasons, you should not hesitate to tell your hosts at the time you are invited.

It is usually acceptable to leave a dinner party thirty minutes or more after the dessert and coffee have been served. You can leave earlier if you need to, but it is better to make it known at the beginning of the evening if you may have to leave early. In most cases, except with close friends, it would be awkward to stay more than an hour after the meal is over. Even so, when you announce that you need to get home, Americans will usually invite you to stay a little longer or ask, "What's your hurry?" This is almost always pure politeness and does not mean that you should stay longer. In taking your leave, it's not necessary or expected that you will mention your desire to reciprocate, although it would not be inappropriate.

Epilogue

The goal of this book has not been to attack or to defend Americans but to explain them, although it's difficult to explain a particular nationality and not seem to be making excuses for them. Be that as it may, as you turn these final pages, it doesn't matter so much whether you think better or worse of Americans but whether you now understand them better. If you do, then this book has done its job: to help you work more effectively with people from the United States.

You should remember, meanwhile, the cautions we have repeated throughout: no two Americans are alike, and neither are any two American workplaces. And nor, for that matter, are any two readers. In the end, you (whoever you are) have to deal with the particular American standing in front of you (whoever he or she may be) in the particular circumstances you find yourselves. With any luck, that person will resemble in some ways — much of the time if not in every instance — the generic American you've been reading about here.

That American is only a type, of course, and you'll never meet a type, only imperfect copies. But there's a good chance you will come across some of the characteristics of that type in the Americans you have to work with. When you do, you will now understand those people better. At the same time you may now also understand your own reactions to Americans better, why some of their attitudes and behaviors strike you the way they do.

You may or may not actually *do* anything with your newfound understanding, applying it, in other words, in day-to-day interactions with Americans. But whether you apply it or not, the nice thing about understanding is that merely in acquiring it, you've already *done* a great deal: you've changed how you see the world.

Bibliography

Althen, Gary. 2003. *American Ways: A Guide for Foreigners in the United States.* Yarmouth, ME: Intercultural Press.

Asselin, Gilles, and Ruth Mastron. 2001. *Au Contraire!: French and Americans.* Yarmouth, ME: Intercultural Press.

Barzini, Luigi. 1983. *The Europeans.* London: Penguin Books.

Birdwhistell, Ray. 1970. *Kinesics and Context.* Philadelphia: University of Pennsylvania Press.

Boorstin, Daniel J. 1976. *America and the Image of Europe: Reflections on American Thought.* Gloucester, MA: Peter Smith.

———. 1965. *The Americans: The National Experience.* New York: Random House.

———. 1958. *The Americans: The Colonial Experience.* New York: Random House.

Bruce, Andy, and Ken Langdon. 2001. *Do It Now!* New York: DK Publishing.

Bryson, Bill. 1999. *I'm A Stranger Here Myself.* New York: Broadway Books.

———. 1995. *Notes from a Small Island.* New York: Avon Books.

Countryman, Edward. 1996. *Americans.* New York: Hill and Wang.

Degler, Carl N. 1984. *Out of Our Past: The Forces That Shaped Modern America.* New York: Harper & Row.

DeVita, Philip R., and James D. Armstrong. 1993. *Distant Mirrors: America as a Foreign Culture.* Belmont, CA: Wadsworth Publishing.

Drozdiak, William. 1998. "The German Status Quo." *Washington Post.* 16 March, A13.

Engel, Dean. 1997. *Passport USA.* San Rafael, CA: World Trade Press.

Faul, Stephanie. 1999. *Xenophobe's Guide to the Americans.* London: Oval Books.

Flamini, Roland. 1997. *Passport Germany: Your Pocket Guide to German Business, Customs & Etiquette.* San Rafael, CA: World Trade Press.

Fox, Grace. 1998. *Office Etiquette and Protocol.* New York: Learning Express.

Fucini, Joseph J., and Suzy Fucini. 1990. *Working for the Japanese: Inside Mazda's American Auto Plant.* New York: The Free Press.

Gannon, Martin J., et al. 1994. *Understanding Global Cultures: Metaphorical Journeys Through 17 Countries*. Thousand Oaks, CA: Sage.

Goldsmith, Charles, and Nikhil Deogun. 2003. "American Lawyer Tom Glocer Hopes to Turn Reuters Around." *Wall Street Journal*. 25 September, B1.

Griessman, B. Eugene. 1994. *Time Tactics of Very Successful People*. New York: McGraw Hill.

Gudykunst, William B., and Stella Ting-Toomey. 1988. *Culture and Interpersonal Communication*. Newbury Park, CA: Sage.

Hall, Edward T., and Mildred Reed Hall. 1990. *Understanding Cultural Differences*. Yarmouth, ME: Intercultural Press.

Hampden-Turner, Charles, and Alfons Trompenaars. 1993. *The Seven Cultures of Capitalism*. New York: Doubleday.

Harper, Timothy. 1997. *Passport United Kingdom: Your Pocket Guide to British Business, Customs & Etiquette*. San Rafael, CA: World Trade Press.

Heller, Robert. 1998. *Motivating People*. New York: DK Publishing.

Hickson, David J., ed. 1997. *Exploring Management Across the World*. London: Penguin Books.

Hickson, David J., and Derek S. Pugh. 1995. *Management Worldwide*. London: Penguin Books.

Hofstede, Geert. 1991. *Cultures and Organizations: Software of the Mind*. Berkshire, UK. McGraw Hill.

Hutner, Gordon. 1999. *Immigrant Voices: Twenty-four Narratives on Becoming an American*. New York: Penguin Putnam.

Ignatius, David. 2002. *Washington Post*. 26 July, A33.

Jones, Howard Mumford. 1968. *O Strange New World: American Culture: The Formative Years*. New York: Viking.

Kammen, Michael. 1980. *People of Paradox*. Ithaca, NY: Cornell University Press.

Kanter, Rosabeth Moss. 1997. *On the Frontiers of Management*. Boston: Harvard Business School Press.

Kim, Eun Y. 2001. *The Yin and Yang of American Culture*. Yarmouth, ME: Intercultural Press.

Kriegel, Robert J., and Louis Patler. 1991. *If it ain't broke . . . break it!* New York: Warner Books.

Langdon, Ken, and Christina Osborne. 2001. *Performance Reviews*. New York: DK Publishing.

Lord, Richard. 1998. *Culture Shock! Succeed in Business. Germany*. Portland, OR: Graphic Arts Center Publishing.

———. 1996. *Culture Shock! Germany.* Portland, OR: Graphic Arts Center Publishing.

Luce, Louise Fiber, and Elise Smith. 1987. *Toward Internationalism.* Cambridge, MA: Newbury House.

Luedtke, Luther. 1992. *Making America: The Society and Culture of the United States.* Chapel Hill: The University of North Carolina Press.

Marquardt, Michael, and Angus Reynolds. 1994. *The Global Learning Organization.* New York: Irwin.

McElroy, John Harmon. 1999. *American Beliefs: What Keeps a Big Country and a Diverse People United.* Chicago: Ivan R. Dee.

McGinn, Daniel, and Stefan Theil. 1999. "Steady Hands: Will the Daimler-Chrysler Combination Succeed? Ask Middle Management." *Newsweek International,* 12 April, 51, 52.

Miller, Stuart. 1990. *Understanding Europeans.* Santa Fe, NM: John Muir.

Mole, John. 2003. *Mind Your Manners: Managing Business Cultures in Europe.* 3rd ed. London: Nicholas Brealey Publishing.

Nees, Greg. 2000. *Germany: Unraveling an Enigma.* Yarmouth, ME: Intercultural Press.

Payer, Lynn. 1989. *Medicine and Culture: Varieties of Treatment in the United States, England, West Germany, and France.* New York: Penguin Books.

Pell, Arthur R. 1995. *The Complete Idiot's Guide to Managing People.* New York: Alpha Books.

Pells, Richard. 1997. *Not Like Us: How Europeans Have Loved, Hated, and Transformed American Culture Since World War II.* New York: Basic Books.

Roces, Alfredo, and Grace Roces. 1994. *Culture Shock: Philippines.* Singapore: Times Editions.

Rosen, Robert, Patricia Digh, Marshall Singer, and Carl Phillips. 2000. *Global Literacies.* New York: Simon & Schuster.

Schorr, Juliet. 1993. *The Overworked American.* New York: Basic Books.

Shahar, Lucy, and David Kurz. 1995. *Border Crossings; American Interactions with Israelis.* Yarmouth, ME: Intercultural Press.

Smith, Perry M. 2002. *Rules and Tools for Leaders.* New York: Penguin Putnam.

Stewart, Edward C., and Milton J. Bennett. 1991. *American Cultural Patterns: A Cross-Cultural Perspective.* Yarmouth, ME: Intercultural Press.

Stewart-Allen, Allyson, and Lanie Denslow. 2002. *Working with Americans: How To Build Profitable Business Relationships.* London: Prentice Hall Business.

Storti, Craig. 2001. *Old World New World: Bridging Cultural Differences.* Yarmouth, ME: Intercultural Press.

Tocqueville, Alexis de. 1984. *Democracy in America.* New York: Penguin Books.

Tracy, Brian. 2000. *The 100 Absolutely Unbreakable Laws of Business Success.* San Francisco: Berrett-Koehler Publishers.

Viscusi, Stephen. 2001. *On the Job: How to Make It in the Real World of Work.* New York: Three Rivers Press.

Wall Street Journal, The Editors of. 2002. *Boss Talk.* New York: Dow Jones and Company.

Wallach, Joel, and Gale Metcalf. 1995. *Working with Americans: A Practical Guide for Asians on How to Succeed with U. S. Managers.* Singapore: McGraw Hill.

Washington Post. 2003. "Names and Faces." 2 February, C3.

Washington Post. 2002. "Fall of Enron." 29 July, A11.

Weiss, Alan. 2000. *The Unofficial Guide to Power Managing.* Foster City, CA: IDG Books Worldwide.

Yardley, Jonathan. 1999. *Washington Post,* 6 June, Book World, 2.

Index

About the Author

Craig Storti is a nationally known figure in the field of intercultural communications and cross-cultural adaptation and is the author of several widely used books in the intercultural field:

- *The Art of Crossing Cultures*
- *The Art of Coming Home*
- *Cross-Cultural Dialogues*
- *Figuring Foreigners Out*
- *Old World/New World: Americans and Europeans*

He has more than twenty-five years of experience training businessmen and women, academics, diplomats, civil servants, and foreign aid workers in undersanding and working effectively with people from other cultures. and diverse backgrounds. As a trainer and consultant, he has advised Fortune 500 companies on international joint ventures and expatriate/repatriation issues, led cross-cultural workshops for international agencies and nongovernmental organizations on four continents, and assisted numerous corporations and government agencies to better manage global teams and a multicultural workforce. His clients include

- Nike
- Exxon Mobil
- Best Buy
- British Telecom
- Pfizer
- FedEx
- Target
- The United Nations
- U.S. Department of State
- Federal Aviation Administration
- NASA
- FBI
- The University of Chicago
- Tulane University
- Vanderbilt University

Craig Storti is also a well-known speaker and has written for a number of national magazines and major newspapers, including *The Washington Post,* the *Los Angeles Times,* and the *Chicago Tribune.* He has lived nearly a quarter of his life abroad — with extended stays in Muslim, Hindu, and Buddhist cultures — and speaks French, Arabic, and Nepali.